ALIGNED

CRISTIN DICKERSON, MD

ALIGNED

How Patients, Physicians, and Employers Are
Working Together to Transform Healthcare

Advantage | Books

Published by Advantage Books, Charleston, South Carolina.
An imprint of Advantage Media.

ADVANTAGE is a registered trademark, and the Advantage colophon is a trademark of Advantage Media Group, Inc.

Printed in the United States of America.

10 9 8 7 6 5 4 3 2 1

ISBN: 978-1-64225-717-5 (Paperback)
ISBN: 978-1-64225-716-8 (eBook)

Library of Congress Control Number: 2023920794

Book design by Analisa Smith.

This publication is designed to provide accurate and authoritative information in regard to the subject matter covered. It is sold with the understanding that the publisher is not engaged in rendering legal, accounting, or other professional services. If legal advice or other expert assistance is required, the services of a competent professional person should be sought.

Advantage Books is an imprint of Advantage Media Group. Advantage Media helps busy entrepreneurs, CEOs, and leaders write and publish a book to grow their business and become the authority in their field. Advantage authors comprise an exclusive community of industry professionals, idea-makers, and thought leaders. For more information go to **advantagemedia.com**.

To all those fighting the daily battle to educate and empower Americans about better and more affordable ways to acquire healthcare.

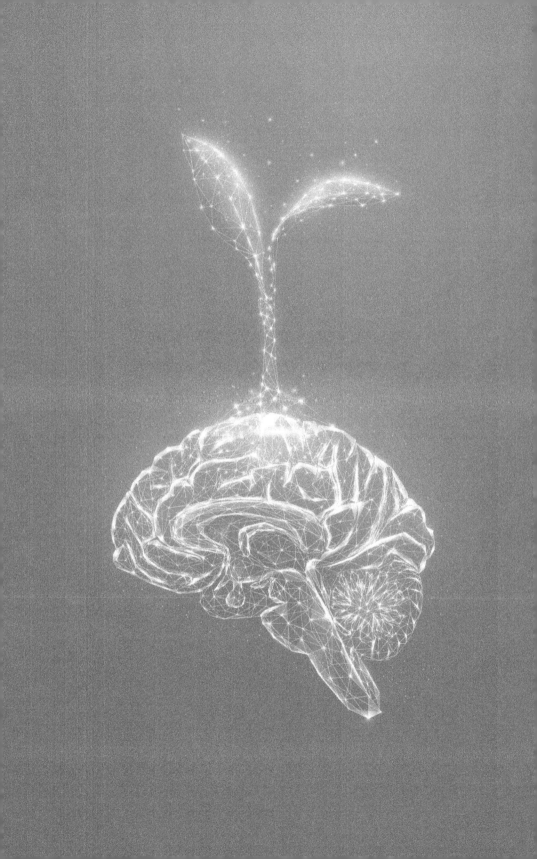

CONTENTS

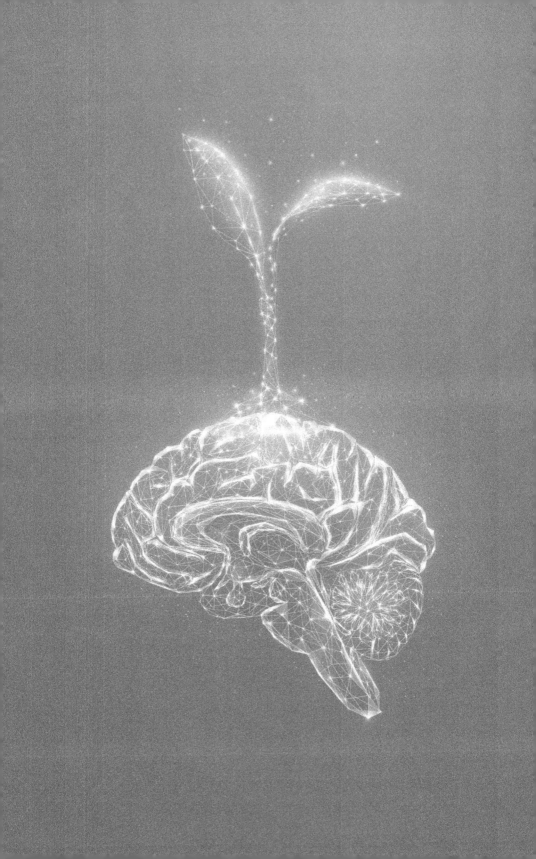

ACKNOWLEDGMENTS

Without Stephen Swope (my husband and the money guy), Catherine Dickerson Kight (my sister and our in-house counsel), and Lee Ann Moore (our COO and my friend since college), this book and Green Imaging would not exist.

Many thanks to those creating new healthcare ecosystems and health plans where solutions like Green Imaging can gain the market share to leverage large volumes of exams for better pricing and mitigate friction points in dealing with the economics of healthcare: Dave Chase, Sean Schantzen, Brian Klepper, Nelson Griswold, Carl Scheussler, Joe Lamantia, Darrell Moon, and Chris Skisak.

Additional thanks go to the other creative healthcare solution founders brave enough to create change and fight the daily battles we face challenging the status quo: Zak Holsworth, Juliet Breeze, Sean Kelley, Taylor Rogers, Paula Muto, and Deb Ault.

Importantly, tremendous thanks to the enlightened benefits advisors, employers, and HR staff members who are embracing change, educating, and supporting Americans who deserve great care on a daily basis.

Finally, thanks to my mom for modeling compassionate professionalism, my dad for instilling in me at an early age that women can achieve their dreams, my husband for his true partnership, my sister for making life more fun and mitigating risk for our company, and Lee Ann Moore for helping me get Green Imaging to the next level.

INTRODUCTION

A gentleman from Amarillo, Texas, was in need of two MRIs, one of the mid-back and one of the low-back. His doctors referred him to an imaging center that was affiliated with a hospital, and it was expected that he would have the imaging done there. So far, his story sounds similar to most medical experiences, right? A patient goes to the doctor, the doctor provides next steps, and the patient follows instructions, never even thinking that there are other options.

Our patient, however, had a high-deductible healthcare plan, with an annual $10,000 deductible. This means he had to pay for medical services out of pocket until he spent that dollar amount. He had learned to check pricing for any medical procedure, so he contacted the medical facility his doctor had recommended. When he inquired about the price of this imaging, he learned that these two procedures would cost $11,000 if he used his insurance. When he negotiated a self-pay price—meaning, he'd pay cash out of pocket—the hospital was able to reduce the cost to $9,000. This difference in price was not substantially helpful to our patient; however—and this is the first key takeaway of the book—*there are two prices on procedures in a hospital system.* The self-pay price will likely always be less; however, any money paid this way will not count toward a patient's

3

annual deductible/maximum out-of-pocket. Sounds like an impossible situation, doesn't it?

Mr. Easton wasn't satisfied at all with the hospital system's pricing. When he pressed the staff and tried to negotiate a more affordable out-of-pocket price, he was very politely denied. They reassured him, however, that all was well; they could arrange a payment plan, wherein he could enroll and *self-pay* over time. Astounded that the staff had actually offered debt as a hopeful solution, Mr. Easton thanked them and hung up. He was smart, knew he had options, and set out to find the best one.

When he contacted us at Green Imaging, the same images, with the radiologist's interpretation, cost one total price of $950. The most shocking aspect of what you're about to learn is not that medical facilities charge tens of thousands of dollars; we all know that, and we're conditioned to accept it. The really appalling part is how much *less* you'll find they can cost.

My name is Dr. Cristin Dickerson, radiologist and owner and founder of Green Imaging. The concept for Green Imaging's business model was formed in adversity, as many innovative ideas are. A private equity firm had acquired my husband's company. When they restructured, Stephen, a very successful real estate broker, was let go. At a point of needing "something new," he suggested opening an imaging center. This started us on a journey of investigating all that needed to be done in the state of Texas to undertake such an endeavor. We quickly realized it would put us $3 to $4 million in debt. That was not at all appealing, so we rejected that option, but the idea had rooted, and we were determined to find a solution.

At that time, Travelocity and similar sales models were emerging. The concept was to resell existing resources that were being underutilized. In Travelocity's case, they provide customers discounted rates on un-booked hotels, rental cars, and the like. I explored options for a similar model for imaging, and what I learned was encouraging.

The radiology group I had founded was interpreting exams for many local imaging centers. This meant even though patients had their imaging done at Imaging Facility A, the staff there did not interpret the imaging or report what the images actually demonstrated for the patient. Instead, Facility A sent the images to us for interpretation. Many of these imaging centers were at 50 percent capacity or less. What if I tapped that unused resource?

As my research bore out, radiologists are not considered referrers but instead are classified as consultants in the laws that prohibit self-referral. Because of this, we are allowed under the Stark Laws—laws governing physician self-referral—to lease imaging centers in a way other physicians and other entities cannot. Thus, the model for Green Imaging emerged.

Stephen was our front and back office that first year. As we found success and built our team, it became a wonderful opportunity to grow a family business. Over twelve years, we have been blessed to work with nieces, nephews, a sister-in-law, a cousin, and our son.

My sister, Catherine Dickerson, is Green Imaging's in-house counsel and my left-hand woman (I am left-handed). She is now one of the most experienced direct contracting attorneys in healthcare and a staunch risk mitigator for our company. Lee Ann Moore, a friend from college, has become our COO. She has brought years of corporate-world experience to Green Imaging and "polished up the details." Catherine, Lee Ann, and I are the "Green Imaging Road Crew," the front line for marketing Green Imaging.

In spite of the fact that our team now has over forty members, this "family business" still maintains a family culture. The level of attention and care that comes from that mindset has made all the difference in our patients' experiences. The best compliment I have received on behalf of our team is that kindness is expressed in their voices.

Throughout my four years of medical school, five years of residency, and twenty-eight years in practice, one recurring theme consistently emerges and has accelerated: the traditional healthcare system is producing less healthy patients with greater healthcare costs and debt.

It was during my two-term presidency of the fifty-physician Diagnostic Clinic of Houston, where I oversaw a self-funded health plan, that I began to have the very first ideas for this book—but I wasn't there yet. In 2011, in partnership with my husband Stephen, I put my then-fifteen years of medical knowledge together with the business of healthcare. Instead of building new imaging centers, we crafted a model where we could offer high-quality medical care for thousands of dollars less by letting patients pay for medical services directly. This is referred to as a "direct-pay" model, sometimes interchangeably called a self-pay model of health coverage.

Don't let the term "self-pay" throw you off. Like our patient with the $10,000 deductible, most of us are already self-paying for healthcare. As functionally uninsured patients, most members never meet their deductible, and many are paying crippling amounts to have a healthcare plan, but their plan doesn't cover their specific healthcare needs.

Supporting this whirlwind financially are the employers who are left responsible for the lion's share of their employees' health premiums. Many are feeling more trapped and overwhelmed with each approaching year because of rising costs. There seems to be no relief at all available to them.

On yet another side of the dilemma are the doctors. They may want to concentrate on high-quality patient care, but they're distracted by the crippling financial requirements needed to stay in business. EMR (electronic medical record) requirements and insurance entities with little medical knowledge and training are dictating what happens in their exam room.

Most affected, however, are the patients. To have the "security" of health coverage, the consumer submits to the rules of the insurance companies—but those insurance companies are not really looking out for the patient's best interest. The whole infrastructure, if you will, has become something of a vacuum, and untold millions of dollars get sucked into administrative costs rather than actual patient care. The result is higher cost to the patient for the same or less service.

Kaiser Family Foundation puts out these statistics in their article, "Americans' Challenges with Healthcare Costs":

> About half of US adults say they have difficulty affording healthcare costs. About four in ten US adults say they have delayed or gone without medical care in the last year due to cost, with dental services being the most common type of care adults report putting off due to cost.
>
> Those who are covered by health insurance are not immune to the burden of healthcare costs. About one-third of insured adults worry about affording their monthly health insurance premium, and 44 percent worry about affording their deductible before health insurance kicks in.[1]

---

1   Alex Montero, Audrey Kearney, Liz Hamel, Mollyann Brodie, "Americans' challenges with healthcare costs," Health Costs, Kaiser Family Foundation, July 14, 2022, accessed September 13, 2023, https://www.kff.org/ health-costs/issue-brief/ americans-challenges-with-health-care-costs.

Healthcare debt is a major burden for a large number of Americans. About four in ten adults (41 percent) report having debt because of medical or dental bills, including debts owed to credit cards, collections agencies, family and friends, banks, and other lenders to pay for their healthcare costs. A disproportionate share of Black and Hispanic adults, women, parents, those with low incomes, and uninsured adults report having healthcare debt.

Americans are having to choose between their health and putting food on the table. As a result, in many cases, people with legitimate healthcare go without care until their circumstances become dire. This type of experience is becoming more and more the norm, but incongruent with the nonattention patients are getting, their costs continue to skyrocket.

What if there were a secure, simplified system of service and payment that eliminated the middleman, lowered prescription costs, and put employer and employee dollars to better use? How about saving thousands per year in outgoing expenses? Wouldn't it make more sense to relieve doctors of financial strain so that they can exclusively care for their patients? Let's add 24/7 personal care from a patient's primary care physician as part of this plan.

Sounds like an interesting fantasy, something impossible to actually accomplish? This healthcare concept is more realistic and achievable than you might guess. In fact, we're about to show you that this way of caring for your health is already a reality for hundreds of thousands of individuals and families, and nationally, its momentum is growing.

Providing quality services to patients who otherwise couldn't afford them is one of my life's goals. Another is my passion for spreading the word that patients, employers, and doctors have innovative, nontraditional healthcare coverage options. That's what I will show you in this book.

So where do we start?

If we do not fully understand the processes that have brought us to this point of needing reform, we honestly cannot make that reform. So let's start right there, with recognizing and outlining the underpinning problems in the current healthcare models.

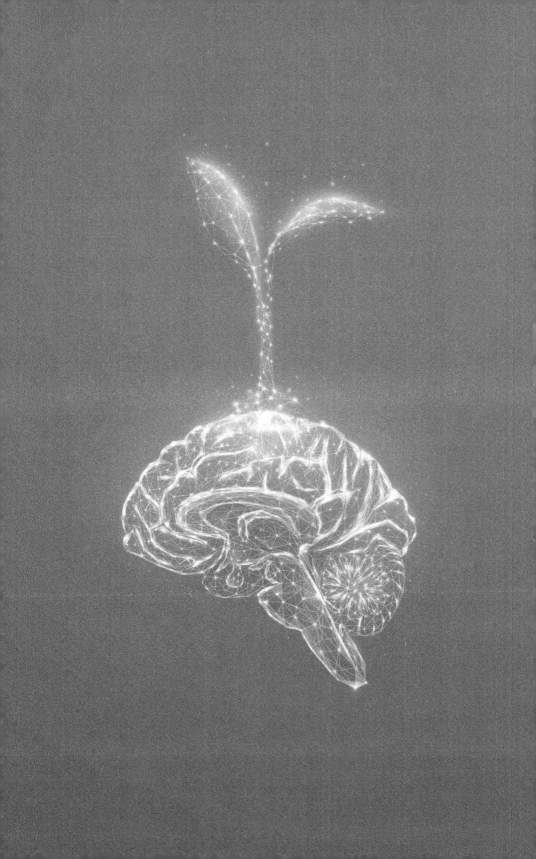

PART 1

Traditional Healthcare

Where the most expensive place to get an MRI is down the hall from your doctor, and no one tells you there are other options.

CHAPTER 1

Underpinning Problems in Current Healthcare Models

Most of us who deal with the healthcare system on any level come to understand that something is wrong with the way things work. When we try to focus on the problem, however, it's hard to really pinpoint how it is out of balance. When my team and I began operating within that system, we could clearly see that the root of the problems lay in current healthcare models, which almost exclusively revolve around traditional health insurance coverage. However, healthcare and health insurance are two very different things.

Healthinsurance.org defines traditional health insurance coverage in this way:

> Health insurance—also referred to as medical insurance or healthcare insurance—refers to insurance that *covers a portion* of the cost of a policyholder's medical costs. *How much the insurance covers*, and how much the policyholder

pays via copays, deductibles, and coinsurance, *depends on the details of the policy itself*, with specific rules and regulations that apply to some plans.[2]

To paraphrase this definition, traditional health coverage is applied for through an insurance provider who pays part of a patient-consumer's health expenses, while they—and/or their employer—pay the rest. When traditional healthcare coverage is established, we see these three major players involved:

The Patient-Consumer: A patient-consumer may apply for health insurance independently, but they typically obtain a plan through employment. Most patient-consumers only know of the traditional healthcare model, so they feel that an employer who offers one of the traditional health insurance brands is offering the best plan for their healthcare needs.

Likewise independent patient-consumers, who could more easily take advantage of creative insurance options, often gravitate toward big-name companies rather than newer, more-innovative models. Stuck in the traditional healthcare mindset, they willingly place themselves in the mainstream system.

The Employer: An employer has several options for the health coverage they offer their employees. They can offer one of the major insurance networks through traditional insurance (fully-funded), they can take on some risk (level-funded), or they can rent the network and purchase a catastrophic stop-loss policy and assume full risk (self-funded).

Although there are ways to save enormous amounts of money with some nontraditional options, to attract candidates, employers often stick with one of the major insurance networks. The employer

---

2   Healthinsurance.org, "What is health insurance and why do we need it?" accessed September 13, 2023, https://www.healthinsurance.org/glossary/health-insurance/.

feels they are offering the best health package, and like the patient, they are often unaware that there are other options.

The Primary Care Physicians and Specialists: These healthcare providers will undoubtedly be called upon at some point to administer care to the patient. To do that, very simply, they must get paid for their service. In an effort at meeting the patient where they are, doctors accept the traditional insurance plans and, somewhat blindly, also move into the mainstream healthcare system.

The Mainstream/Hospital Healthcare System

The mainstream healthcare system largely revolves around hospital affiliation. This means mainstream insurance companies will cover the procedures done at the hospitals that accept their insurance. Sounds like a good thing, doesn't it? "Hospital affiliation" speaks to high-quality care. Everyone, from the doctors to the hospitals to the insurance companies involved, gives the impression that using hospital-affiliated health services is the only way to get high-quality attention.

This is patently false. Nontraditional health plans can offer the same top-quality care at a fraction of the cost. One of the most difficult underpinning problems of the traditional healthcare model is the mindset that there's a safety in having health insurance because the insurance company will cover medical expenses. Is this true, however? If you really consider the plan design that mainstream healthcare typically structures, many of us are already paying the majority of our own health expenses out of pocket.

Before we get into those details, though, why would the hospital system *not* be the best place, overall, for care?

Mainstream/Hospital Healthcare Costs

As insurance holders, patients trust in the network touted by their insurance company. They certainly believe that their doctor is advising them correctly. Yet they frequently experience huge and unexpected medical bills.

Let's take, for example, a patient that Kaiser Health News highlights:[3] Dani Yuengling, a thirty-five-year-old young woman, had a regular mammogram that returned some traumatizing news. Her doctor, working within the hospital system, ordered a breast biopsy at a hospital-affiliated facility. Mrs. Yuengling had a high-deductible health insurance plan, with a $6,000 deductible. Trying to avoid a full $6,000 debt, she did her due diligence and called the hospital facility prior to her biopsy to discuss cost. The staff somewhat unhelpfully told her that would depend on which type of biopsy she needed.

Determined, she did some research on her own and saw that there were two procedures for her breast biopsy. Trying to err on the side of caution, she chose the more expensive of the two procedures. With that decided, she opened the hospital system's online calculator to get an approximate out-of-pocket cost. Part of that process was entering her insurance information, but the program would not accept her entries. Thinking that the worst-case scenario would be having to pay for the biopsy out of pocket, she finally tried the calculator without entering any insurance information into the system at all, as if she were an uninsured, cash patient. She was finally given an estimated cost of $1,400. This was a manageable price for her. Relieved, she moved forward with the biopsy.

---

3   Lauren Sausser, "The $18,000 breast biopsy: when having insurance costs you a bundle," August 23, 2022, KFF Health News, accessed September 13, 2023, https://khn.org/news/article/bill-of-the-month-breast-biopsy-with-insurance.

When the procedure was complete, Mrs. Yuengling received a bill in the mail stating a total cost for her biopsy nearing $18,000. She couldn't believe it, and frankly, she was concerned as to how she would pay for her part of it. Instead of the $1,400 she had budgeted for, she now owed her full high deductible of $6,000. The biopsy was complete at this point, so all she could do was call the hospital to discuss this outrageous bill. As if they were presenting her with a great gift, the hospital reduced her out-of-pocket cost by 36 percent. She was stuck with a $3,306.29 bill that she hadn't planned on and did not understand.

What nobody told her was that she never had to go through the hospital system in the first place. She could have scheduled that same biopsy at a private, doctor-owned radiology practice. Had she brought her prescription to Green Imaging, for instance, we could have performed that same biopsy, including the professional fees, typically for less than $2,000.

Doctors in a hospital system are usually financially incentivized to use other services provided by that system. Even though the services are "covered" by the big-name insurance companies, they are priced so disproportionately high that a routine scan can cost a patient their full deductible/out-of-pocket maximum. Once that happens, patients typically continue in this system without considering further cost of care because "the insurance pays for everything now." Do they, really?

True, if all of your care is in network, you as the patient may not have to pay more for medical services in that calendar year. However, when you start collecting from the insurance company for subsequent medical issues, you may quickly be flagged as high risk. If you're independently insured, this higher-risk status will cause increases in your insurance costs. If you're insured through your employer, your entire group of insured coworkers may be impacted by this costly care. If you've ever dealt with an insurance application, you know that high-risk circumstances mean you will be paying high dollars in insurance premiums each month.

Compounding the issue, when employers sponsor healthcare for their employees, they are the ones who largely face these hefty annual increases. To balance their budgets when such financial stress hits, employers negotiate a lesser premium. This inevitably results in less coverage and/or higher deductibles for the whole employee group. As everyone is paying more and a raise would certainly help, another consequence kicks in: when the cost of the health plan increases, typically wages stagnate in tandem.

CHAPTER 2

Sicker Patients Yield More Profit

In the hospital system, the sicker the patient is, the more money doctors make on referrals for specialists, imaging exams, testing, drugs, surgeries, and the like. Perhaps you or a family member have personally experienced the following scenario:

Mr. Stevens is scheduled for a yearly physical at the end of the month. During a strenuous game of tennis, one week prior to his visit, he overextends his right elbow, and it's becoming concerning. He decides that he will simply bring the matter to his doctor's attention during his physical. When he does, the staff reschedules a separate visit to the office to "take a look" at the issue.

Mr. Stevens is perplexed; he's sitting right there with his arm extended. Why not just "take a look" right then and there?

The truth is, if the doctor just "adds on a service," they will not be paid equally for that additional care. Now, in all fairness, this isn't just a money grab. Like any other financial enterprise, if there is not adequate payment for services, they might go out of business. Doctors spend a significant amount of time ordering referrals, labs, imaging, reading reports, and deciding on the best subsequent course of care. To get paid for all that energy, they may require the patient to return to the office both for that secondary examination and yet again to receive their results.

When Mr. Stevens finally got back to see his doctor for that secondary issue, he was completely bewildered when the nurse asked the very same preparatory questions all over again. Why would this be needed? Is the patient so insignificant that there is no record of their prior answers? Not at all. The reason is that the traditional healthcare system is designed to pay for each complaint. This is when levels of care and the EMR come into play.

The EMR is not built to be doctor friendly; it is built to maximize payment for the level of care provided and thus increase what hospital systems are paid. The data entered into the EMR is "coded" through the CPT and ICD-10 coding systems. To bill for higher-level exams, specific guidelines must be met to apply these codes. The "repeat questions," or *review of systems*, is applied redundantly to meet the maximum complexity of care for that visit.

CPT stands for current procedural terminology, and the American Medical Association (AMA) defines the purpose of the CPT coding system as follows: "The CPT® coding system offers doctors across the country a uniform process for coding medical services that streamlines reporting and increases accuracy and efficiency."[4]

---

4   American Medical Association, "CPT® purpose & mission," accessed September 13, 2023, https://www.ama-assn.org/about/cpt-editorial-panel/cpt-purpose-mission.

Similarly, billing relies on the AMA's ICD-10 system, which "is a system used by physicians to code all medical diagnoses and procedures for claims processing."[5]

The AMA goes on to say this about the ICD-10 system: "As a HIPAA-mandated code set, all covered entities (physicians, other healthcare providers, payers and clearinghouses) must use ICD-10 to be in compliance with HIPAA."[6]

So for healthcare providers in the traditional healthcare system to get paid, they must use the CPT codes that identify each illness/symptom. In addition, they must bill through the ICD-10 system. Here's the kicker: the AMA—which only *11 percent* of practicing physicians believe truly represents them[7]—holds the billing rights on these codes. Anyone needing to use them, from individual healthcare providers to hospital systems to the US government, must pay high fees to the AMA to do so.[8]

Moreover, a sicker patient is eligible for referrals for additional care. The more doctors in the traditional healthcare system refer patients to affiliated hospital-system testing facilities, specialists, and so on, the more doctors can receive financially for the high level of care required.

---

5   American Medical Association, "ICD-10," accessed September 13, 2023, https://www.ama-assn.org/topics/icd-10#:~:text=Centers%20for%20Medicar-,International%20Classification%20of%20Diseases%2C%20Tenth%20Revision%20(ICD%2D10),and%20procedures%20for%20claims%20processing.

6   American Medical Association, "ICD-10 Overview," accessed September 13, 2023, https://www.ama-assn.org/practice-management/claims-processing/icd-10-overview#:~:text=As%20a%20HIPAA%2Dmandated% 20code,required%20to%20comply%20with%20HIPAA.

7   Linda Girgis, "Is the AMA really the voice of physicians in the US?" Physicians Weekly, June 9, 2015, accessed September 13, 2023, https://www.physiciansweekly.com/is-the-ama-really-the-voice-of-physicians-in-the-us/.

8   Robert Gabriel, "Why do I have to pay a fee to use CPT codes?" Microwize, December 14, 2022, accessed September 13, 2023, https://microwize.com/why-do-i-have-to-pay-a-fee-to-use-cpt-code/.

Let's be clear about the laws concerning referrals; the American Society of Anesthesiologists describes these laws in detail:

> The Federal Anti-Kickback Statute (AKS) (see 42 U.S.C. § 1320a-7b.) is a criminal statute that prohibits the exchange (or offer to exchange), of anything of value, in an effort to induce (or reward) the referral of business reimbursable by federal healthcare programs. Examples of prohibited kickbacks include receiving financial incentives for referrals, free or very low rent for office space, or excessive compensation for medical directorships. Other kickbacks include waving copayments, either routinely or on a selective case-by-case basis. The Centers for Medicare and Medicaid Services (CMS) claims that kickbacks have led to overutilization and increased costs of healthcare services, corruption of medical decision making, steering patients away from valid services or therapies and unfair, non-competitive service delivery. Possible penalties for violating the AKS include fines of up to $25,000, up to five years in jail, and exclusion from Medicare and Medicaid care program business.

> The physician self-referral laws (Stark Laws) (see 42 U.S.C. § 1395nn) are a set of United States federal civil laws that prohibit physician self-referral, specifically a referral by a physician of a Medicare or Medicaid patient to an entity providing designated health services (DHS) if the physician (or his or her immediate family member) has a financial relationship with that entity. Although the financial penalties may be even greater than with the AKS, these are non-criminal charges. Penalties for violations of Stark Law include denial of payment for the DHS provided, refund of monies received by physicians and

facilities for amounts collected, payment of civil penalties of up to $15,000 for each service that a person "knows or should know" was provided in violation of the law, and three times the amount of improper payment the entity received from the Medicare program, exclusion from the Medicare program and/or state healthcare programs including Medicaid and payment of civil penalties for attempting to circumvent the law of up to $100,000 for each circumvention scheme.[9]

It's clearly against the law for doctors to receive payment or "kickbacks" for referring a Medicare or Medicaid patient for medical treatment. However, the Affordable Care Act (ACA) stepped in to muddy the waters. With a claim of ensuring quality care, the ACA created a *bonus system*, which "*[increases] payments to Medicare Advantage plans based on a five-star rating system.* The goal of the program is to encourage plans to compete for enrollees based on quality."[10]

So with the ACA's effort at providing quality care, doctors essentially began receiving a quality rating, and their referrals counted toward this rating. John Joseph puts out an excellent summary of this phenomenon:[11]

---

9   American Society of Anesthesiologists, "Anti-kickback statute and physician self-referral laws (Stark Laws)," accessed September 13, 2023, https://www.asahq.org/quality-and-practice-management/managing-your-practice/timely-topics-in-payment-and-practice-management/anti-kickback-statute-and-physician-self-referral-laws-stark-laws#:~:text=The%20federal%20Anti%2DKickback%20Statute,by%20federal%20health%20care%20programs.

10 Jeannie Fuglesten Biniek, Anthony Damico, Tricia Neuman, "Spending on Medicare advantage quality bonus payments will reach at least $12.8 billion in 2023," Kaiser Family Foundation, August 9, 2023, accessed September 13, 2023, https://www.kff.org/medicare/issue-brief/spending-on-medicare-advantage-quality-bonus-payments-will-reach-at-least-12-8-billion-in-2023/.

11 John Joseph, "Do primary care doctors get paid for referring patients to specialists?" Quora.com, accessed September 13, 2023, https://www.quora.com/search?q=john%20joseph%20while%20the%20pcp.

The government has set up specific programs for medical practices seeing Medicare patients. The goal of the programs (visit The Quality Payment Program to learn more) is to ensure Medicare receiving practices are providing quality care to patients. *One aspect of that program is to ensure continuity between your PCP and specialist. How they perform in this area has a direct impact on whether or not the PCP and specialist get paid the same rate for a particular service in the future.* If the providers have a poor score, they may be penalized by getting paid less per procedure through Medicare. If they do well, they may receive an increase payment for a procedure.

So no, money is not directly handed over to a physician for their Medicare or Medicaid referral. They are, however, incentivized to give and take referrals within the hospital system to achieve a rating which will lead to bonuses.

Most employed physicians' take-home pay is indirectly based on revenue generated for the system. It doesn't take long to realize that the sicker a patient is, the more money comes into the doctor's pocket. This begins to misalign the interests of the patient and those of the doctor, and many doctors never realize this is happening to them. It's a way of doing business that is natural to the business world, but it's at odds with the Hippocratic oath.

Upon graduation, a doctor swears to do no harm to their patients. That would naturally include financial harm and any harm to a patient's state of mind. Burdening them with copay after copay, removing them from work to keep appointments, and playing into a system that causes financial strain are very often causing them harm.

CHAPTER 3

Nontransparent Pricing

arlier we introduced Mrs. Yuengling, who was confronted with an $18,000 biopsy, resulting in her full out-of-pocket deductible coming due. Why was her bill so much higher, even after she called the hospital for pricing? Shouldn't the bill have at least been close to the $1,400 estimate she determined through the hospital system's calculator? This is where indeterminate, or nontransparent, pricing comes into play.

Let's say the radiologist began this procedure and found an additional lump, or the patient began bleeding excessively. Whatever additional medical needs arise during that biopsy will be added to the patient's bill without alerting them of the add-on. Since complications can happen during a procedure, this is one of the reasons hospitals cite as an inability to quote accurately. Another is that, even if the physician is employed by the hospital, their specific fee, among others, may not be included in the hospital's initial quote.

What often happens when a patient contacts the facility as an anonymous uninsured person seeking cash rates is that a self-pay rate is quoted, oftentimes based on Medicare rates. If they are truly uninsured, this likely would be the cash-pay price of their biopsy. If you recall, Mrs. Yuengling's insurance information kept getting rejected. When she finally managed to get a price, it was as a self-pay consumer, and that price was $1,400. When she was admitted into the hospital facility for her biopsy, her insurance status became known. As if that $1,400 quote never existed, the insurance's contracted rates were charged, resulting in the near-$18,000 total bill.

What if the patient has insurance but simply does not want to use it? Hospitals tell us regularly that if a patient has insurance, it must be used, which is absolutely not true. The Department of Health and Human Services Office for Civil Rights says this in their publication *Health Information Privacy Rights*:

> *Let your providers or health insurance companies know if there is information you do not want to share.* You can ask that your health information not be shared with certain people, groups, or companies. If you go to a clinic, for example, you can ask the doctor not to share your medical records with other doctors or nurses at the clinic. You can ask for other kinds of restrictions, but they do not always have to agree to do what you ask, particularly if it could affect your care. *Finally, you can also ask your healthcare provider or pharmacy not to tell your health insurance company about care you receive or drugs you take, if you pay for the care or drugs in full and*

the provider or pharmacy does not need to get paid by your insurance company.[12]

Clearly, the Health Insurance Portability and Accountability Act (HIPAA) provides the patient the right to withhold protected health information (PHI) from insurance companies and negotiate self-pay pricing. Instead, when the patient enters just a few pieces of PHI into the hospital system, that information is run through claim scrubbing software—or a "scrubber." These programs take the patient's personal information without their permission, and in violation of HIPAA Omnibus regulations, they "find" the patient's insurance status.

Scrubbers were originally intended to locate claims information if an unidentified patient passed away in the emergency room (ER) or a patient provided incomplete insurance information. What they are used for in reality is often as demonstrated in Mrs. Yuengling's case: they check to see if patients have insurance. If they do, the traditional hospital system often quotes a higher price than if they had no insurance. Just the name and date of birth may be enough information to find out if the person has insurance and/or if they can be billed for their medical treatment.

Once a patient is known to have insurance, it doesn't matter if a different estimate was quoted. Touting rules that go directly against HIPAA, medical staff frequently bill a patient's insurance overblown rates just because there is insurance coverage. Then ready or not, that patient is responsible for any copays and deductibles. In this way, *the insurance companies and hospital systems work together to keep dollars flowing liberally among them.*

---

12   Office for Civil Rights, "Health information privacy rights," accessed September 13, 2023, https://www.hhs.gov/sites/default/files/ocr/privacy/hipaa/understanding/consumers/consumer_rights.pdf.

Claim scrubbing software must be subscribed to, and the hospitals spend liberally to have this ability. It's obvious why that is: the exact same procedure when the hospital discovered Mrs. Yuengling's health insurance status afforded them a 92 percent increase in revenue—and that's just one patient.

Bundling and Unbundling Services

When patients come to Green Imaging, we quote them one price for the radiology service they need. This price includes the radiology exam itself, world-class concierge service, the results of their exam interpreted by a radiologist, any medications or contrast needed, and any high-level processing required. So in reality, a patient's single procedure actually takes many services to complete. When all services are combined into one price, it's called "bundling" services.

Now let's say a patient needs a hepatobiliary iminodiacetic acid (HIDA) scan of the gallbladder. This is a nuclear-medicine exam, requiring a gamma camera and radioactive medication. It frequently must be done through the hospital system because many imaging centers don't have the necessary equipment. There will be a price for the scan, the injection, required medication, the radiotracer, the professional interpretation of the patient's results, and the professional component of the injection. When all these services are billed separately, it's called "unbundling."

So if we examine Mrs. Yuengling's case again, we recall that she was quoted a cost of $1,400 for her biopsy. This quote did not contain the fee to perform the biopsy. This, combined with inflated rates through insurance, would ultimately be what skyrocketed her total to $18,000. *The services were unbundled.*

Further, astounding as it is, even if the hospital is in network, *there is no guarantee the performing doctor is*. Most health plans also have higher copays, coinsurance, and deductibles for out-of-network services.

It helps if you do *not* try to see the logic because there really isn't any, except perhaps intentional complexity to confuse consumers.

Barriers to Transparent Pricing

Anyone who has tried to get quick, accurate pricing from any facility in a hospital system knows that it's not for the faint of heart. To price a surgery or procedure accurately, one must know all the services needed, which is another reason why medical facilities get away with outrageous inaccuracies when speaking directly to a patient.

To provide a good-faith estimate, hospital-affiliated facilities should only require the patient's name, date of birth, and exam type. Instead, they're requiring full-on demographics, the patient's order, and even the CPT codes to provide a good-faith estimate. How many patients know the correct CPT codes that correspond with each exam? Maybe 1 percent of patients have that kind of knowledge. Complicating things even more, hospital facilities often refuse to let a third party negotiate on the patient's behalf or obtain pricing for them. Therefore, patients are frequently stymied in their efforts at obtaining that bottom-line price.

Green Imaging offers world-class concierge service, meaning we regularly take on the burden of finding these prices when we assemble a one-price package. Even we, medically trained personnel from a nationally recognized company, get the door of easy, transparent pricing closed multiple times every day. This, by the way, is in direct violation of the No Surprises Act:

Starting in 2022, there are new protections that prevent surprise medical bills. If you have private health insurance, these new protections ban the most common types of surprise bills. *If you're uninsured or you decide not to use your health insurance for a service, under these protections, you can often get a good-faith estimate of the cost of your care up front, before your visit.* If you disagree with your bill, you may be able to dispute the charges.[13]

As the ones shopping for quotes for our patients, we find that barriers of resistance to transparent quotes suddenly appear. Here are the top four barriers we typically face:

1. HOSPITAL SYSTEMS AND INSURANCE PROVIDERS—PARTNERS IN CRIME

The major health insurers typically pay an independent doctor—one not aligned with a hospital system—at or below Medicare rates. In fact, doctors usually sign a sixty-page contract that literally forces them to comply with the insurance network's rules, with little room for negotiation. Hospitals, however, have a different fee schedule that works hand-in-hand with the insurance companies to keep high prices "standard," or expected and accepted.

For example, we regularly come across computed tomography (CT) contrast charges that were billed out through the hospital system at around $20,000. The actual cost of that contrast is about $15, and a fair price, considering the office staff has to make a living, would be closer to $50.

---

13   CMS.gov, Fact sheet, "No surprises: understand your rights against surprise medical bills," January 03, 2022, accessed September 13, 2023, https://www.cms.gov/newsroom/fact-sheets/no-surprises-understand-your-rights-against-surprise-medical-bills.

How do these prices get so out of hand in the mainstream system? Because hospitals and insurance companies work from a completely different set of prices than Medicare, called "the chargemaster." According to the National Academy for State Health Policy, "A hospital chargemaster is the collection of standard list prices for hospital services. Chargemaster rates are essentially the healthcare market equivalent of an MSRP, Manufacturer's Suggested Retail Price, in the car-buying market."[14]

These definitions really do say it all. Every car owner out there knows that the MSRP on a vehicle is drastically marked up. When hospitals have a Medicare-insured patient, they simply accept the Medicare payment. Treatment for insured patients, however, is automatically priced according to the hospital's chargemaster pricing, which, astoundingly, is not regulated by any governing entity. Insured patients will be charged according to any "discounts" off this pricing schedule, and, as we've already demonstrated, that pricing is grossly inflated.

Insurance networks sell brokers and employers on their "discounts" off billed charges, but when the numerator (chargemaster price) can be manipulated upward to offset discounting, the discounts are an illusion.

It used to be very difficult to obtain a hospital's chargemaster rates, but luckily, in January 2021, the laws on hospital pricing transparency became clearer. The Centers for Medicare & Medicaid Services explains the change:

> Starting January 1, 2021, each hospital operating in the United States will be required to provide clear, accessible

---

14   Deb Fournier, Irish Riley, Marilyn Bartlett, "Can we please stop fixating on hospital chargemasters?" National Academy of State Health Policy, accessed September 13, 2023, https://nashp.org/can-we-please-stop-fixating-on-hospital-chargemasters/.

pricing information online about the items and services they provide in two ways:

1. As a comprehensive machine-readable file with all items and services.

2. In a display of shoppable services in a consumer-friendly format.

This information will make it easier for consumers to shop and compare prices across hospitals and estimate the cost of care before going to the hospital. … [Hospitals] may face civil monetary penalties for noncompliance.[15]

We must stop seeing healthcare as a blind tunnel we're required to enter for medical treatment and start seeing it as a negotiable service (most of the time)—like buying a car.

2. HOSPITAL STAFF REALLY DOESN'T KNOW FINAL PRICING

I know this is hard to believe, but the second barrier we encounter when trying to find transparent pricing is that the staff really doesn't know what the cost of a procedure will be. Post-pandemic, for example, we are seeing increasing cases of myocarditis. Let's say one of these patients is scheduled for an echocardiogram, which is an ultrasound of the heart. The patient calls the hospital system to get the price of the procedure, and they are given that price—for an echocardiogram.

That's not the full price, however, because we come back to unbundling. A radiology group typically has an exclusive agreement with the hospital, and there usually isn't too much difficulty learning

---

15   Hospital Price Transparency, Centers for Medicare & Medicaid Services, "Hospital price transparency," accessed September 13, 2023, https://www.cms.gov/hospital-price-transparency.

who that is. There's a cardiology group involved in the echocardiogram interpretation, however, rather than a single radiology group, and this is where things may become confusing. The cardiologist's services will be billed separately from the scan itself. When the patient asks who the cardiologist is who will read the study, however, the medical staff genuinely may not know.

Why not? Because the cardiologists read these types of results in rotation, depending on how they take calls and how they cover the hospital, and there are usually multiple cardiology groups covering a hospital. So if the patient requests the fee of the specific cardiologist who will read their results, the hospital staff really may not be able to provide that information.

3. CITING HIPAA LIMITATIONS

Another frustration we encounter when trying to get accurate pricing for a specific patient's procedure is that some hospital systems immediately state that no third party is allowed to shop on the patient's behalf. They claim HIPAA law prevents them from speaking to anyone except the patient. Again, when we look at the actual language of the rule, we see this is not true:

> The Privacy Rule permits a covered entity, or a business associate acting on behalf of a covered entity (e.g., a collection agency), to disclose protected health information as necessary to obtain payment for healthcare, and does not limit to whom such a disclosure may be made.[16]

---

16 U.S. DEPARTMENT OF HEALTH AND HUMAN SERVICES Office for Civil Rights, "HIPAA, health information exchanges, and disclosures of protected health information for public health purposes," accessed September 13, 2023, https://www.hhs.gov/sites/default/files/hie-faqs.pdf.

Hospitals are actually in violation of HIPAA laws when they refuse to disclose pricing to a patient's advocate. What they're doing is making it more difficult for the patient to get a real self-pay price as advocates are often more educated on the protections in place for these patients.

4. THE DELAY FACTOR

Last but certainly not the least, we come to the delay factor when hospital-system pricing is requested. Staff will stipulate the need for a "reasonable amount of time," up to seventy-two hours, to gather your information.

When someone fears that they are sick or they have been told they need an echocardiogram or a CT scan, seventy-two hours may be an agonizing time to wait. The human psyche in this situation is programmed to seek care, and a patient certainly may not be in a frame of mind to fight for pricing for a serious test. In fact, this patient may need immediate answers and attention. Asking them to wait may well result in "just going ahead and using the system" in an effort at getting relief. It feels like the system is designed to produce this result.

CHAPTER 4

"Nonprofit" Hospitals

S tay with me for just a few minutes here, because we need to become familiar with a few more definitions. What they reveal, I'm certain, will be eye-opening and worthwhile.

The Internal Revenue Service (IRS) defines nonprofit hospitals as follows:

> Charitable hospitals must meet the general requirements for tax exemption under Internal Revenue Code (IRC) Section 501(c)(3) and Revenue Ruling 69-545 PDF ... in addition to the four additional requirements imposed under IRC Section 501(r)(1).

> Section 501(c)(3) organizations must be organized and operated exclusively for specific tax-exempt purposes to be exempt from federal income tax. In addition to being a type of organization that is specifically described within Section

501(c)(3), these organizations must also have the following characteristics:

- No part of their net earnings is allowed to inure to the benefit of any private shareholder or individual.

- No substantial part of their activities can consist of carrying on propaganda or otherwise attempting to influence legislation, and

- The organization should not participate in, or intervene in, any political campaign on behalf of (or in opposition to) any candidate for public office.[17]

To recap, nonprofit hospitals do not have to pay property or income tax because their goals and interests are supposedly motivated by service to the community. Because of this sincere motivation, it is naturally expected that they invest their profits back into said communities.

Where do these bastions of public service come from, however? How do they get funding in the first place to build their nonprofit medical campuses and maintain the economics of such massive business structures?

Customarily, nonprofit hospitals are owned by charitable/religious organizations or nonprofit corporations, such as Catholic Health Systems, Methodist Health System Foundation, or Kaiser Permanente. They function as any hospital business does, meaning they offer medical services and consumers pay for them.

---

17   IRS, "Charitable hospitals - general requirements for tax-exemption under section 501(c)(3). Organizational and operational tests," accessed September 13, 2023, https://www.irs.gov/charities-non-profits/charitable-hospitals-general-requirements-for-tax-exemption-under-section-501c3.

Because these "nonprofit" hospital systems work together with the largest insurance companies, they are leveraged to charge patients astronomical prices. This obviously creates profit. Again, to keep the all-important nonprofit status, it's expected that they put that profit back into their communities by updating their facilities and offering charity care.

When the ACA was instated, however, many people who previously required charity care now had insurance. Yet, we see in a 2021 Johns Hopkins study that for every $100 in total spending, nonprofit hospitals provided only $2.30 of total care to uninsured patients who could not pay for it, while "for-profit" hospitals provided $3.80 to the same demographic.[18]

So, if they are accepting insurance and making enough profit to offer multiple millions of dollars in employment packages to their administrators, how is it that they still qualify for nonprofit status?

In truth, nonprofit hospitals are making multiple millions in profit every year, and many states, such as New York, are regularly funding them. In the city of Houston, every prosperous suburb has a huge, state-of-the-art Texas Medical Center Hospital System campus, surrounded by acres of parking lots that in many cases stay virtually empty. There may be a handful of doctors there on any given day who rotate there infrequently. These hospitals sit on some of the most expensive land in our city, and again, they *are not* subject to taxes. *For-profit* hospitals, owned by investors, must pay millions of dollars in property and income taxes, and their charity numbers are equal to nonprofit numbers.

---

18   Ge Bai, Hossein Zare, Matthew D. Eisenberg, Daniel Polsky, Gerard F. Anderson, "Analysis suggests government and nonprofit hospitals' charity care is not aligned with their favorable tax treatment," Healthaffairs.org, April 2021, accessed September 13, 2023, https://www.healthaffairs.org/doi/abs/10.1377/hlthaff.2020.01627.

If we strip this down to its true reality, many nonprofit hospitals have become neatly packaged real estate investment trusts. They use their profit to occupy the most valuable land, and they deny those cities millions in tax dollars that would truly make a difference in their communities.

CHAPTER 5

Overarching Roles

One of the more dramatic developments in the overall healthcare system has been the empowerment of nonphysician healthcare professionals. Don't misunderstand me; healthcare professionals are necessary. Personally, when my children were small, I preferred seeing the nurse practitioner in our pediatrician's office. I felt she was more sensitive to the children and took more time with their care. She was particularly effective because she operated her practice *under the doctor's oversight.* She regularly checked with the pediatrician if there were questions or issues.

Even though many states recognize healthcare professionals as independent medical practitioners, it's been my experience that having carte blanche to practice without any physician oversight creates room for errors. Here is an example.

In Houston, a Texas Medical Center hospital offers an "undiagnosed" breast clinic, where women may voluntarily go for second opinions. This facility is staffed by a nurse practitioner. This practitioner frequently repeats the ultrasound and renders different opinions than highly trained radiologists who are also trained in interpreting mammography and have experience correlating a mammogram with the ultrasound. The lack of someone qualified to interpret the ultrasound in conjunction with the mammogram is a critical omission in breast imaging.

When the patients return to my clinic for an annual mammogram the following year, that outside opinion is included in their charts. A radiologist never correlates that practitioner's findings with the mammogram.

I have a real problem with this, and I regularly challenge these alternate results. One of the cornerstones of my practice is engaging in a peer-review process, consulting with several qualified radiologists regarding any question in an interpretation. As a mammographer for twenty-seven years, a large portion of my career has been spent reading mammograms and breast ultrasounds and performing breast biopsies. I cannot tell you the number of times I have read a patient's scan, received a different opinion from the nurse practitioner, implemented this peer-review process, and then alerted the referring physician to our findings. Whether the patient took our advice or that of the clinic really depended on who they believed. Unless the patient knew the details of each reading, they could easily accept the nurse practitioner's interpretation, consider themselves safe from cancer, and neglect necessary follow-up care.

This brings us back to the frame of mind, or a person's psyche, when they are ill or frightened by a possible medical condition. The majority want to believe the less-intimidating diagnosis. When that diagnosis comes from a well-known hospital, they often cling to the easier-to-handle analysis. There is no way of knowing how many patients never received crucial follow-up because they were given a different interpretation that brought on a false sense of security.

I fully understand that these statements may anger some nurse practitioners, especially those with thriving practices. Again, I maintain that, although they may provide outstanding care, the degree of medical education and training doctors undergo better prepares them to make final recommendations regarding a patient's health. If we consider the above two breast ultrasounds according to the education and training of those who might render an opinion, we can clearly see that a licensed radiologist is better qualified to render the final medical judgment:

NURSE PRACTITIONER (NP) *AMERICAN ASSOCIATION OF NURSE PRACTITIONERS (AANP. ORG)*	RADIOLOGIST *UNIVERSITY OF MEDICINE AND HEALTH SCIENCES (UMHS)*
• Complete a Bachelor of Science in Nursing (BSN); must be a registered nurse (RN); usually takes four years. • Complete an NP-focused graduate master's or doctoral nursing program; usually takes two to three years, but accelerated programs offer the BSN and MSN in three to five years. • Successfully pass a national NP board certification exam.	• Complete an undergraduate degree, which usually takes four years. • Complete four years of medical school. • Complete a one-year internship. • Complete an additional four years of residency training in Diagnostic Radiology. • After completing high school, on average it will take thirteen years to become a radiologist. • Successfully pass the American Board of Radiology's (ABR) certification exam.

Secondary care providers are much-needed partners in an industry that certainly needs their skills and compassion. They provide a cost-effective way for hospitals and patients alike to expedite treatment. To actually override a doctor's order, without the oversight of another qualified physician, in my experience, is not in the best interest of the patient, the doctor, the healthcare professional who renders the opinion, or the hospital system where this empowerment takes place.

Misaligned Incentives

As we continue discussing the issues related to traditional health insurance models, it's clear that the insurance companies themselves are one of the biggest problems. Why? Quite simply, we assume that a mainstream company, such as Blue Cross Blue Shield, Humana, or Cigna, with their compelling commercials and reassuring sales pitches, is actually taking care of us. They are not. They are focused on, and taking care of, their investors.

In 2011, the Obama administration enacted the "80/20" rule, also known as Medical Loss Ratio (MLR). This rule allows only 20 percent of profit from the premiums health insurance companies collect to be taken as profit. The other 80 percent must be reinvested back into quality improvement activities and healthcare costs, meaning the actual payouts for their insured clients' medical needs. Again, all of this sounds like a move in the right direction, and yet we see it was not.

The administration claimed that the 80/20 rule held insurance companies accountable and saved billions of dollars in premiums for Americans. In reality, the insurance companies did not become motivated to invest that 80 percent back into "healthcare costs." Instead, they became interested in maintaining their profits. To do this, they simply raised their rates to keep up, thereby increasing overall healthcare costs—exactly the opposite of what the ACA claimed to achieve.

When we take a look at "big-house" (traditional) health insurance brokers, once again, we see misaligned incentives in traditional healthcare models. The more healthcare costs, of course, the higher the broker's commissions will be on sales. If that's not bad enough, brokerage houses are given "confidential" bonuses based on reaching a target volume of policies sold for that company. These bonus offers are brazenly designed to entice brokers into selling the respective insurance companies' healthcare products to employers and employee-consumers, even when they may not be the best option.

"Set sail for Bermuda," says insurance giant Cigna, offering top-selling brokers five days at one of the island's luxury resorts.

Health Net of California's pitch is not subtle: a smiling woman in a business suit rides a giant $100 bill like it's a surfboard. "Sell more, enroll more, get paid more!" In some cases, its ad says, a broker can "power up" the bonus to $150,000 per employer group.

Not to be outdone, New York's EmblemHealth promises top-selling brokers "the chance of a lifetime": going to bat against the retired legendary New York Yankees pitcher Mariano Rivera.

In another offer, the company, which bills itself as the state's largest nonprofit plan, focuses on cash: "The more subscribers you enroll ... the bigger the payout." Bonuses, it says, top out at $100,000 per group, and "there's no limit to the number of bonuses you can earn." [19]

These certainly are amazing extras, but what are the brokers' incentives? To get the most appropriate and cost-effective healthcare plans into people's lives? I'd argue that their main incentive is to reach these bonus goals, whether the product is the best one for their client or not.

There is a need for quality brokerage services in the healthcare industry. Benefits advisors associated with Dave Chase's Health Rosetta, Carl Schuessler's Mitigate Partners, Nelson Griswold's NextGen Healthcare, and a handful of "Innovation Centers" associated with traditional brokerages distinguish themselves by honestly applying their knowledge and expertise to a situation and receiving a fair compensation for their efforts. These types of advisors' incentives are typically aligned correctly with the needs of their clients.

BONUS PARTICIPANT TESTIMONIAL

Taylor Rogers | Benefits Advisor

I was working for a big-house consultancy before we broke off and started our firm. We focus on the niche of helping employers cut out all the layers of middlemen that both increase costs and delay access to care.

For example, we have a client who operates in an industry

---

19 Marshall Allen, "Insurers hand out cash and gifts to sway brokers who sell employer health plans," NPR, February 20, 2019, accessed September 13, 2023, https://www.npr.org/sections/health-shots/2019/02/20/694719998/insurers-hand-out-cash-and-gifts-to-sway-brokers-who-sell-employer-health-plans.

with razor-thin margins. Nearly 90 percent of their operational expense is tied to compensation and benefits—extremely high cost of human capital. Reducing health plan costs by 20–30 percent in an environment like that has a material impact on the valuation of the business. When that business goes to transact, adding $2 million back to their bottom line at a 5× EBITDA (earnings before interest, taxes, depreciation, and amortization) multiple, the result is $10 million of deal value to the seller.

In addition to the financial lift, their plan was headed in such a negative direction that many of their people had put off basic healthcare. Our care navigation team came across many members who had delayed critical procedures because they couldn't afford the out-of-pocket expense under their prior plan.

We basically hit restart on designing an employer's benefits program. In many cases, we move them to an optimized, self-funded plan; this requires a plan administrator who is conflict-free and working solely for the interests of our client.

We create plan-document language that allows the plan sponsor to fulfill their fiduciary responsibility to plan members; we optimize vendor contracts and ensure their stop-loss contracts are adequately transferring risk for the appropriate time period; we add direct provider agreements for surgical bundles, outpatient care, cancer management, maternity management, and so on; then we layer on the care navigation to connect members to the appropriate solutions when they need them. Care navigation is what separates good performers from great ones.

What type of results do we customarily achieve? Fast-forward to when the company with razor-thin margins implemented our program: not only did the company see drastic savings, but several employees were also able to have those overdue procedures taken care of, and they paid nothing out of pocket.

As we assess underpinning problems with current healthcare models, these obvious questions must be asked to ascertain if the current system is working: Is the traditional healthcare dollar well spent? Has the mainstream healthcare system impacted participants in a positive way or negative?

Let's move forward to see exactly how this system has impacted the three primary parties that are subjected to participation: the doctor, the employer, and the employee or patient-consumer. Because none of these ideas move forward if there isn't a doctor to provide care, let's start our study there.

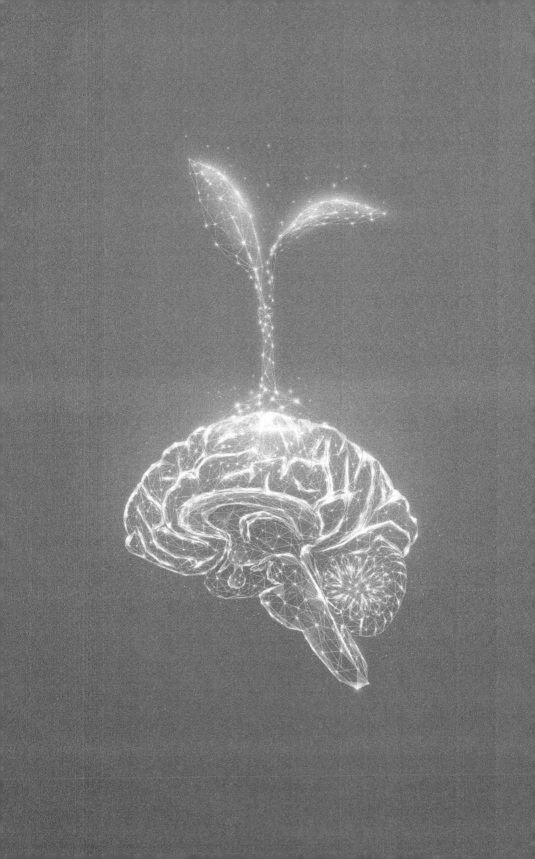

PART 2

The Impact of Mainstream Healthcare on Participants

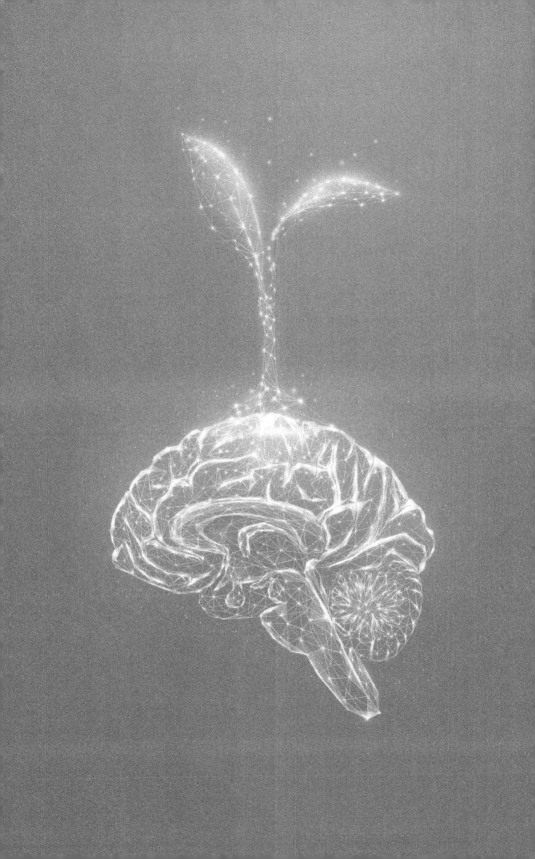

CHAPTER 7

The Impact of Mainstream Healthcare on Doctors

n 2018, MedicalProtection.org released an astounding report about their member physicians. Their survey of more than six hundred UK members revealed that "85 percent have experienced mental health issues, with common issues being stress (75 percent), anxiety (49 percent) and low self-esteem (36 percent). A third of respondents (32 percent) have had depression during their medical career, while one in 10 (13 percent) stated they had experienced suicidal feelings."[20]

The survey also found that of the respondents who reported having mental health issues, 76 percent cited heavy workload, 70 percent cited long working hours as contributing factors to those issues, 60 percent of those surveyed felt their mental health impacted

---

20 Medical Protection, "85% of doctors have experienced mental health issues, reveals Medical Protection survey," November 14, 2018, accessed September 13, 2023, https://www.medicalprotection.org/uk/articles/85-of-doctors-have-experienced-mental-health-issues-reveals-medical-protection-survey.

their ability to concentrate, and 36 percent felt it impacted their empathy toward patients.

The high levels of scrutiny and regulation that a physician faces resulted in negative impacts on 54 percent of respondents' mental health, and "41 percent of those affected did not discuss their issues with anyone, with 58 percent of those believing they did not need support, and a quarter (24 percent) feeling there is a stigma attached to mental health issues."[21]

Since the time of this report, the COVID pandemic redefined what many doctors knew to be sound medical care, and many are still reeling from its effects. I honestly could write another book about all of the "moral injury," physical, mental, emotional, and even spiritual stressors that impact doctors in our current healthcare climate. In the interest of time and focus, I'll limit commentary to the top seven business elements that I see as impactful to physicians.

Inability to Provide Personal Standard of Care

If you recall, Mr. Stevens—our patient who overextended an elbow playing tennis—tried to talk to his primary care physician about his injury. We explained how levels of care and the EMR come into play so that the doctor must reschedule to get paid for that additional care. These limitations keep patients and doctors in a perpetual loop of seeking and giving medical services.

If this pressure to be paid does not detract from a doctor's instinct to "care for" the patient, this next hindrance will: the fifteen-minute appointment churn they must keep up with to achieve financial benchmarks expected by their employers.

---

21   Ibid.

In 1992, Medicare adopted a system for paying doctors based on RVUs, or "relative value units." Essentially, RVUs are used to measure the "relative level of time, skill, training, and intensity required of a physician to provide a given service. RVUs therefore are a method for calculating the volume of work or effort expended by a physician in treating patients. A well-patient visit, for example, would be assigned a lower RVU than an invasive surgical procedure."[22]

A complex formula is used, but it basically comes down to overall office efficiency. In this "efficiency" system, only fifteen minutes ended up being allotted for well visits. This means that Medicare's new way of assessing care would only pay the doctor for fifteen minutes of time to care for a generally healthy patient. If they were trying to explain an overextended elbow or anything else during that visit, there just wasn't the time to provide the care.

Kaiser Health News provides an excellent summation of Medicare's change to RVU efficiency:

> The typical office visit for a primary care patient was pegged at 1.3 RVUs, and the American Medical Association coding guidelines for that type of visit suggested a fifteen-minute consult.

> Private insurers, in turn, piggybacked on Medicare's fee schedule, said Princeton health economist Uwe Reinhardt. Then, in the 1990s, he said, "managed care came in and hit doctors with brutal force."

---

22   Merritt Hawkins, "RVU based physician compensation and productivity," AMN Healthcare, July 16, 2021, accessed September 13, 2020, https://www.amnhealthcare. com/siteassets/amn-insights/whitepapers/rvu-based-physician-compensation-and-productivity.pdf.

Doctors who participated in managed care networks had to give insurers discounts on their rates; in exchange, the insurers promised to steer ever more patients their way.

To avoid income cuts, Reinhardt said, "doctors had to see more patients; instead of doing three an hour, they did four."[23]

So not only did doctors' time with actual patients funnel down because Medicare would only authorize fifteen minutes of care, but the amount of money they were being paid for each visit had also been discounted even further. Besides that, doctors spend 50 percent of their time on the EMR,[24] so they're actually spending even less time caring for the patient. This puts them in a perpetual state of anxiety that demands more and more business to survive.

The patient, unfortunately, is left feeling rushed and possibly unable to fully explain their medical needs. The doctor is left feeling detached, sometimes impatient, because of the forced time constraints that they are under.

Prior Authorizations

Ron Barshop, a direct primary care (DPC) advocate, provides these statistics[25] on doctors' ability to provide quality care with the restrictions of prior authorizations:

---

23   Roni Caryn Rabin, "15-Minute visits take a toll on the doctor-patient relationship," This KHN story was produced in collaboration with USA Today, April 21, 2014, accessed September 13, 2023, https://khn.org/news/15-minute-doctor-visits/.

24   Kelly Young, David G. Fairchild, "Half of physician time spent on EHRs and paperwork," NEJM Journal Watch, September 6, 2016, accessed September 13, 2023, https://www.jwatch.org/fw111995/2016/09/06/half-physician-time-spent-ehrs-and-paperwork.

25   Ron Barshop, "Primary Care Cures," LinkedIn, October 2022, accessed September 13, 2023, https://www.linkedin.com/posts/ron-barshop_ama-prior-authorization-pa-physician-survey-activity-6982234448339628032-56BV.

- 91 percent of physicians agree: prior authorizations negatively impact #clinical outcomes

- 88 percent describe the burden as high/very high

- Docs each complete 41 prior authorizations weekly—13 hours of staff time is devoted to just this

- 40 percent have MAs devoted just to prior authorizations

- 51 percent report prior authorizations interfere with employees' job performance

- 82 percent report patients abandon treatment waiting, and 73 percent of declines are reversed in time.

He adds, "I met a pediatrician who told me insulin that worked well 8 years to treat T1 diabetes was denied by a non-whitecoat. That kind of sums up prior authorizations."

As a refresher, a *referral* is an order from a patient's primary care physician for them to receive medical services from a specialist or secondary provider. A *prior authorization* is when the patient's insurance provider will review the case and decide if the procedure is medically necessary.

One patient, a well-insured medical director for a client of Green Imaging, found himself in a dire situation because of a prior authorization. He was having severe pain in the right lower abdominal area. He could not get to his primary care physician, and the discomfort was so acute that he went directly to an urgent care center. Even though he carried one of the "top-tier" plans with Aetna, he was left struggling in this condition, while urgent care waited for his insurance to authorize the care.

He finally just left, went home, and crawled into bed. Lying there, however, he couldn't fall asleep or find any relief. The next morning, finally remembering our association, he sent me a text asking if I could get him in for an exam to see what was going on. We took him as soon as possible and discovered his gallbladder was obstructed and infected and he required surgery. Untreated gallbladders with this level of disease can cause sepsis, which is a serious blood infection. If left untreated, sepsis can lead to severe illness or even death. In spite of this, the traditional system had this patient suffering in a waiting-room chair while hour after hour went by in wait for that prior authorization.

Abandonment of the "Business of Medicine"

There is a business side to practicing medicine, and rather than work through it, doctors have abdicated the duty of "the business of medicine" to the mainstream system. When that happens, the ethics of medicine begins to be diluted by the drive for profit.

If a doctor is financially free and removed from the hyper-rush, fifteen-minute system, what will the focus be when entering a patient's exam room? Likely, it will be what it should have always been: building a relationship and finding ways to make and keep the patient healthy. This is exactly what the patient wants, so incentives are aligned.

When the patient is looking for care and attention, but the doctor knows there will only be about fifteen minutes, the focus is no longer on getting and keeping the patient healthy. The incentive is to turn this appointment over and move to the next patient. Patients can sense this, and they often feel bewildered, devalued, and confused, especially if they are paying out of pocket for this treatment.

If the ethics of medicine are removed or buried in an administrative quagmire, there is no longer a free market. Unfortunately, this is exactly what has already happened in the mainstream healthcare system. Part of the reason for that loss is because doctors do not properly handle the business of medicine.

Imbalanced Pay Structures

Patient-consumers often have the erroneous idea that doctors are extremely wealthy and that "all the money" that seems to be disappearing into healthcare oblivion is going into doctors' pockets. The truth is, if doctors knew what the hospital system was charging for their services, compared to what they are actually taking home, there would likely be a revolt.

During the height of the pandemic, I knew doctors who served in the ICU. These physicians were literally getting their wills in order and going weeks without seeing their children because they had a sincere desire to serve their patients. This is what makes it so egregious that the ones who made substantial profit during that time were in the mainstream system: insurance companies, hospitals, pharmaceutical companies, and the private-equity consolidators of healthcare—*not* the doctors and nurses.

In fact, according to the National Library of Medicine, "doctors' net take-home pay (that is income minus expenses) amounts to only about 10 percent of overall healthcare spending."[26]

Where, then, is the money going? Health News takes that question on directly:

> The ratio of doctors to other healthcare workers is now 1:16, up from 1:14 two decades ago. Of those sixteen workers for every doctor, only six are involved in caring for patients—

---

26   Timothy B. Norbeck, "Drivers of healthcare costs: a physicians foundation white paper - first of a three-part series," National Library of Medicine National Center for Biotechnology Information, accessed September 13, 2023, https://www.ncbi.nlm.nih. gov/pmc/articles/PMC6179628/.

nurses and home health aides, for example. The other ten are in purely administrative roles.[27]

So we see that it's actually the hospital administrators, whose benefits packages swell up into the millions per year, who create the biggest wage deficit in the industry.

The *Not-So* Balanced Budget Act of 1997

To fully understand how the Balanced Budget Act of 1997 is impacting healthcare today, let's take a look at what the Act was designed to accomplish:

> The Balanced Budget Act, signed into law by the President on August 5, 1997, contains the largest reductions in federal Medicaid (CMS) spending in Medicaid since 1981. The legislation is projected to achieve gross federal Medicaid savings of $17 billion over the next five years and $61.4 billion over the next ten years.[28]

Considering we've spent nearly seven chapters discussing outrageous healthcare costs, "balancing budgets" in healthcare sounds like a positive, doesn't it? Let's think about that, however. Medicaid spending was cut by $17 *billion* in the first five years of this program.

---

27   Heather Ross, "The great healthcare bloat: 10 Administrators for every 1 U.S. doctor," Health News, updated on January 30, 2019, accessed September 13, 2023, https://www.healthline.com/health-news/policy-ten-administrators-for-every-one-us-doctor-092813.

28   Andy Schneider, "Overview of Medicaid provisions in the Balanced Budget Act of 1997, P.L. 105-33," Center on Budget and Policy Priorities, accessed September 13, 2023, https://www.cbpp.org/sites/default/files/archive/908mcaid.htm#:~:text=The%20Balanced%20Budget%20Act%20signed,over%20the%20next%20ten%20years.

This did not make healthcare *costs* go down; it made what was available in payment for the soaring services limited by another $17 billion.

Let me be quick to add that in 1997 when this went into effect, there was a genuine need for Medicare and Medicaid payment expansion toward the primary care sector of medicine.

The real problem is that when specialty medical services were assessed, such as radiology and cardiology, they took a reduction in payments for services. Since then, year after year, CMS has continued slashing funds for medical specialties. While the cost of living rises by leaps, and specialty medical equipment ascends into the million-dollar range, CMS persists in bleeding a well that is already dry.

In radiology specifically, independent imaging centers and physician practices have taken huge payment cuts for imaging services. This is in spite of the fact that state-of-the-art equipment is needed, which often costs millions of dollars to purchase and maintain. At the time of this writing in fact, helium, which is necessary for an MRI machine to function properly, is in worldwide global shortage. Costs are skyrocketing, while allotted medical reimbursement for that service continues to decline.

Making matters worse was the pandemic. In Texas, one of the less restrictive states, we were limited by the governor to "essential imaging studies" only during the shutdowns. Fifty percent of my company's business dried up almost instantly. Post-pandemic, our reschedule rates were in the 30 percent range for the majority of 2021. Medicare was only paying about $237 for an MRI. The cost to maintain versus the dollars coming in made business virtually unsustainable. In fact, we had to shut down the discount MRI center we owned in Houston altogether because, in order to keep the doors open, we would have had to charge what everyone else charged. It didn't make sense to continue it.

The result of all of this is that private-equity-backed groups are buying up the independent centers because they are struggling, literally, to keep the lights on. These private-equity-backed groups might purchase ten imaging centers at a time; therefore, they have leverage when they go to the insurance companies, and they can contract better rates to make up for the Medicare/Medicaid population. They also consolidate existing contracts from these centers, enabling them to collect the highest reimbursement possible.

An independent imaging center has no negotiating power with the insurance companies. In fact, they are often lucky to even get a contract with the major insurance providers. UnitedHealthcare told us for years that they did not need any new imaging centers in the Houston area. Their panels were closed, so we could not even get a contract. With this kind of pressure and financial loss, independent centers are left with little choice but to sell, and private-equity-backed groups are corralling them and quietly moving them directly into the mainstream system at much higher cost.

In summary, the Balanced Budget Act of 1997 led to unbalanced budgets for many specialty services. This directly correlates to more independent medical-specialty facilities coming under the mainstream system.

Overbearing Noncompete Rules

Most people are familiar with noncompete agreements from observing the sales world. When a salesperson signs on with a company, let's say for computer sales, they typically sign an agreement stating that if they leave, they will not take any trade secrets or clientele with them.

The hospital systems also require noncompete agreements; however, these noncompetes are so overbearing that they tie the hands of their doctors. I've known radiologists who practice with private-equity-backed radiology groups who are required to sign noncompetes that restrict them from practicing within sixty miles of a facility they staff. If you look at a map of the area, that noncompete has effectively cut them off from practicing at all because that leaves them nowhere to go.

Attorneys often scoff at these noncompetes, explaining that they can be fought in the legal system. This may be true, but in the real world, hospitals and medical groups have deep pockets while individual physicians do not. They can—and will—cripple a lone physician who is in violation of those agreements by tying them up in hundreds of thousands of dollars in ongoing legal fees.

Dr. Juliet Breeze, founder and CEO of Next Level Urgent Medical, tells of finding herself unable to practice to her standard of care in a major hospital system. She wanted to (gasp!) listen and take time with her patients, and it was impossible with the demands of the administrative team. She tried to extricate herself after four-and-a-half years of family practice and found that, because of her noncompete, she couldn't practice within one hundred miles of her previous mainstream facility. Uprooting her family to relocate her practice would create an undue burden on the rest of her family, so she was effectively cut off from practicing at all.

Fortunately, Dr. Breeze was able to get right back on her feet. She began running her husband's orthopedic practice, building it into a thriving, sought-after medical group. It was so successful, in fact, that they were able to turn around and sell it to a hospital system.

Not all doctors are that innovative, nor do they have the resources to bounce back so dramatically. Instead, sadly, they submit and become part of the system.

Inappropriate Acute Care

From my perspective as a doctor, perhaps the most frustrating pattern I observe is when patients forgo primary care until their complaint escalates into the need to seek acute care, or ER treatment.

Because of prohibitive costs, people are neglecting healthcare maintenance, and the very worst possible result occurs: When the need for healthcare arises—any type of healthcare—they go straight to the ER or closest urgent care facility. In some cases, the care is not even appropriate. ER staff are not trained—nor should they be—to take care of coughs, colds, and minor conditions. Those types of illnesses should be taken care of by primary care physicians.

Clearly, the impact mainstream healthcare has had on doctors, in many cases, comes in severely lacking. From the way physicians in this system must treat their patients to the way they are treated by insurance companies and hospital administrations shows a misalignment of attitudes and functionality.

As we move into chapter 8, we will switch our focus to the employer. As we progress, pay particular attention to how doctors and employers must work together (with patients) to break out of the mainstream healthcare system.

The Impact of Mainstream Healthcare on Employers

Without a doubt, the greatest impact on employers when dealing with the mainstream healthcare system is cost. When we examine traditional health insurance companies and who really pays for healthcare premiums, we see that it's actually the employers who get hit with the highest expenditures. In 2023, the Kaiser Family Foundation released their findings on Health Insurance Premiums and Worker Contributions. Let's recap their results:[29]

- In 2023, the average healthcare premium for an individual was about $8,435

- Of that $8,435, *employers paid $7,034 (83 percent)*, and employees paid $1,401 (17 percent)

---

29   "2023 Employer Health Benefits Survey," Kaiser Family Foundation, October 18, 2023, accessed December 2, 2023, https://www.kff.org/report-section/ehbs-2023-summary-of-findings/#figurea.

- In 2023, the average healthcare premium for a family was about $23,968

- Of that $23,968, *employers paid $17,393 (73 percent)*, and the employees paid $6,575 (27 percent)

So we see that employers regularly take on the largest costs for healthcare. The insurance companies, on the other hand, are making record profits yet continue to raise rates in order to maintain that profit margin. Catering to the big-name hospitals rather than the patients is part of this mindset. They loudly proclaim that they are offering discounts, and they are sure to use the buzzwords "deep discounts" to get everyone's attention.

I can't tell you how many employers have told me, "We get amazing discounts from Blue Cross Blue Shield" (or Cigna, Humana, etc.). They are perplexed when we question this "discount." If there is no set numerator, a discount means nothing. So where do the health insurance companies get their pricing in order to provide this discount?

They rely on the hospital systems' chargemaster rates. Again, these rates are not regulated; therefore, as we've already discussed, hospitals can set them at practically any figure they want. For the insurance company to provide a "deep discount," the hospital system simply gives chargemaster rates an even steeper *increase*, and the profits, for them, are maintained—or climb higher.

Fiduciary Duty

Staggering costs tend to distract and blind employers to a critical facet of their responsibility: employers partially funding health insurance premiums—which is typical—have a fiduciary duty. This means they have a moral and legal requirement to handle their employees' money carefully and act within their best interest.

In 2019, the school board of the School District of Osceola County, Florida, found itself in a head-on collision with fiduciary duty. A fairly substantial wage increase was completely eclipsed by increases in members' out-of-pocket costs for their Cigna plan. The teachers' union realized that healthcare costs for their members were disproportionately high.

Imagine this: your company gives notice of a 5 percent wage increase beginning next quarter. You're happy about this; the money will come in handy; possibly, you plan a new purchase with the extra income. Instead, just when the wage increase should take effect, the entire amount—all of it—is wiped out by increased out-of-pocket cost for health insurance.

This is just what happened to these educators. The deductible for their health plan increased to $4,000, with a 50 percent coinsurance—meaning members would be responsible for up to $6,000 in max out-of-pocket expense. They couldn't even afford to use the plan because the deductible was so high.

Discontentment brought the district to a full investigation, where they discovered massive inconsistencies on the part of their benefits manager, Gallagher Benefits. According to their case filing,[30] "The district is also seeking punitive damages for Gallagher's breach of fiduciary duty and fraud." The lawsuit cited examples: "Two heart surgeries that should have each cost roughly $220,000 were approved and performed for $2 million while prescriptions selling less than $20 over the counter were approved for $250."

---

30   Gabrielle Russon, "Osceola Schools' lawsuit against insurance consultant can go on, judge rules," Floridapolitics.com, June 29, 2022, accessed September 13, 2023, https://floridapolitics.com/archives/536170-osceola-schools-lawsuit-against-insurance-consultant-can-go-on-judge-rules.

"Under the self-funded model of employer-sponsored health insurance, the school board remained responsible for the portion of the healthcare costs not paid for by the member," the lawsuit said. "Cigna's failure to conservatively approve treatment and failure to negotiate competitive prices for prescriptions and medical procedures forced the School Board to grossly overpay healthcare providers and pharmacies."[31]

This lawsuit really does encapsulate the responsibility of the employer to handle healthcare and employee funds responsibly. Prices and conditions can, and should, be negotiated.

Employers who do their fiduciary duty and take the time to investigate coverage options for their employees find that direct-contracted healthcare is typically the most affordable, and more importantly, the most effective way to maintain good health.

Employers need their personnel physically and mentally present on the job.

Providing an excellent health coverage package for them and their families results in less time away from work and greater ability to excel in their positions.

How We Got Here

At this point, we can clearly see the fault lines in the insurance-hospital system, but you might be wondering how employers gained the responsibility of providing health insurance in the first place. As we mentioned, employers attract quality candidates by offering top-name

---

31   Gabrielle Russon, "Osceola Schools blast consultant's 'greed' in health plan choice," Floridapolitics.com, December 1, 2021, accessed September 13, 2023, https://floridapolitics.com/archives/476848-osceola-schools-blast-consultants-greed-in-health-plan-choice/.

insurance plans. Interestingly, the practice of enticing employees, both to take positions and to remain at a company, is not a modern concept. In fact, this is how employer-sponsored healthcare began.

During World War II, President Roosevelt signed Executive Order 9250, which, among other things, froze wages. At the same time, workers were leaving their jobs to go serve in World War II. Employers everywhere were in crisis. They needed a full workforce, so they devised creative ways to make their companies attractive. Rather than offer the higher wages which Executive Order 9250 restricted, they offered health insurance packages. Thus, the "benefits package" began.

In 1943, the concept of employer-sponsored healthcare was all but cemented in place when the War Labor Board, together with the IRS, granted a 100 percent tax exemption to employers offering healthcare. Employer-sponsored healthcare was here to stay, and the population eagerly adopted this healthcare model.

In the late 1980s through the early 1990s, we see the beginning of our current inflated healthcare costs. It was known as the Death Spiral, and journalist Gabrielle Smith put out an ideal description in her blog article:

> When an employee's cost to participate in the employer plan gets too expensive, the healthiest employees begin to drop off the employer plan in favor of more affordable individual policies. This causes the remaining small employer risk pool to become "sicker," resulting in higher insurance premiums on renewal the following year.

Then, the process repeats. Again, the employer reduces benefits to maintain costs, more healthy employees drop off, and the rate goes up the following year.[32]

In 2010, the ACA was passed. In an effort at balancing out coverage availability for the employee-consumer, the Obama administration passed the Patient Protection and Affordable Care Act (P.L. 111-148), which would "require US citizens and legal residents to have qualifying health coverage."[33]

Those mandates worked in reverse, causing a dramatic drop in people electing to have health insurance. The death spiral worsened. Eligible members in individual group pools decreased, causing another surge in prices for the employer and the employee.

Although in 2019 the Trump administration abolished those mandates, the penalties for not offering healthcare are still in place. Therefore, when health insurance premiums continue to skyrocket, employers are faced with large annual increases. To offset these increases, they search for plans that are less expensive; in the traditional system, the less expensive the plan is, the higher the deductible will be, and the death spiral continues.

---

32 Gabrielle Smith, "The complete history of employer-provided health insurance," People Keep, March 31, 2021, accessed September 13, 2023, https://www.people-keep.com/blog/the-complete-history-of-employer-provided-health-insurance.

33 "Summary of the Affordable Care Act, Patient Protection and Affordable Care Act (P.L. 111-148)," Individual Mandate, Requirement to have coverage, Kaiser Family Foundation, April 25, 2013, accessed September 13, 2023, https://www.kff.org/health-reform/fact-sheet/summary-of-the-affordable-care-act/.

CHAPTER 9

The Impact of Mainstream Healthcare on Employees

As difficult as the doctor and employer have it as they wade through the mainstream system, the worst impact lands on patients. Why? Very simply, they are not getting the care they need. According to CNBC, "54 percent of Americans say they've delayed care for themselves in the past year because of cost, and another 23 percent delayed care for more than a year for the same reason. Meanwhile, 10 percent of Americans with children under the age of eighteen have delayed care for a dependent or child because of financial issues."[34]

These patients are in the mainstream system; therefore, almost every doctor visit and subsequent complication are overpriced to begin with, and then they must pay for it out of pocket because of

---

34 Shawn M. Carter, "Over half of Americans delay or don't get healthcare because they can't afford it—these 3 treatments get put off most," CNBC, April 3, 2010, accessed September 13, 2023, https://www.cnbc.com/2018/11/29/over-half-of-americans-delay-health-care-becasue-they-cant-afford-it.html.

high copays, deductibles, coinsurance, and out-of-pocket maximums. The result is functionally uninsured employee-patients.

Functionally Uninsured

Patients who carry employer-sponsored health coverage, as we've already discussed, pay about 17 percent of the premium. Add to that, copays, coinsurance, and anything the plan deems as "not a covered expense," which are also paid by the employee.

The copay is a fixed amount that is paid at the time a member receives medical services or gets a prescription filled, in advance of reaching the maximum out-of-pocket defined by the plan.

The deductible is the amount a member is required to pay before the health insurance starts to cover defined benefits.

Coinsurance is the percentage of costs a member must pay for a covered healthcare service after the deductible is met (e.g., 20 percent).

Maximum out-of-pocket is the most a member is required to pay for covered services in a plan year. After this amount is spent on deductibles and coinsurance for in-network care and services, the health plan pays 100 percent of the costs of covered, in-network benefits. There are usually higher copays, deductibles, coinsurance, and out-of-pocket maximums for out-of-network care.

As a refresher, a plan that includes a high deductible will typically cost less on a monthly basis. If the plan carries a high monthly premium, typically there will be a lower deductible before insurance kicks in. When those high premiums are presented to employees and employers alike, it's easy to see why high-deductible plans are a popular choice: They simply cost less up front.

Let's take the Easton family, for instance, whose youngest child is asthmatic. Mr. Easton holds the family insurance. His employer only offers a high-deductible healthcare plan, which carries a yearly deductible of $4,300 and a monthly premium of $440. There are no exceptional provisions for asthma, so they must pay out of pocket for the child's asthma equipment, medications, and doctor visits, until they reach $4,300. Then, their insurance will kick in, and the family's medical concerns will be at least partially covered. This is in addition to the $440 monthly premium.

In January 2021, CBC News published an article alarmingly titled "Most Americans couldn't cover a $1,000 financial emergency, survey finds." In it, they report that "fewer than 4 in 10 Americans have enough money set aside to cover an unexpected $1,000 expense, such as a trip to the E.R. or car repairs, according to a new survey."[35]

The Eastons fall into this category. Yet they pay a whopping $3,000 per year, or about $250 per month, on asthma treatments and supplies.

If you do the math, even paying $250 every month out of pocket, they will not reach their high-deductible threshold. Unless another health concern arises in their family—which they sincerely hope does not—the Eastons will pay $690 per month for their health needs ($440 in premiums and $250 in medical expenses), and they'll never get to take advantage of the insurance they're paying for. This is a prime example of a family being functionally uninsured.

Because patients like the Eastons see their doctor less often, their health issues become more complex. As a result, their path back to health is more involved, and oftentimes, they wait until they're feeling so ill that an ER visit is the only answer. Now, their expenses will be mountainous—a catch-22 if ever there was one. *People are already*

---

35   Kate Gibson, "Most Americans couldn't cover a $1,000 financial emergency, survey finds," MONEYWATCH, CBS News, January 11, 2021, accessed September 13, 2023, https://www.cbsnews.com/news/financial-emergency-savings-americans-cover/.

paying for their own healthcare, unless something catastrophic happens, such as an emergency surgery or a life-threatening disease.

To compound the problem, we see the following three additional burdens on patients using the mainstream system.

1. UNNECESSARY CARE

Unnecessary care occurs when a patient presents with an illness that cannot be cured or it is impractical to provide standard treatment, yet an aggressive treatment plan is ordered.

For instance, my mother is eighty-five years old, and she has a touch of dementia. We know this is vascular related on the basis of prior migraine headaches and not really progressive. She happened to be changing doctors, and I knew during the course of this change exactly what would happen: the new doctor would see the condition in her chart, ignore the fact that she's already been diagnosed and she, along with her family and care team, had chosen how to manage it, and they'd go ahead and order a $10,000 to $30,000 dementia workup *when there is no present cure*. It is a pointless endeavor, wastes time and money, and takes a toll on the patient and the family.

Now, let's assume that the same eighty-five-year-old woman has a three-millimeter breast cancer. There are aggressive treatments for this type of cancer that can be effective. To take this particular patient through those treatments, however, might reduce her quality of life for the remainder of her time on the earth. In the best interest of this particular patient, a better course of care might be medications to mitigate the disease for as long as possible as opposed to the more radical options that are appropriate for younger, stronger patients. Nevertheless, the more aggressive course is standard in the mainstream system.

2. SELF-DIAGNOSING TO AVOID MEDICAL BILLS

A popular comedian, Sebastian Maniscalco, tells his story of having dry hands and googling some possible causes. After several hours of research, he was traumatized, and with a sinking heart, he called his doctor. His search results had convinced him that he had contracted an incurable disease and was, in fact, dying.

Although comical, the skit illustrates a true problem with patients performing Google searches on their symptoms and referring to medical sites such as WebMD: colossal errors can take place when they perform self-diagnoses.

A lung nodule does not necessarily mean cancer, but a patient could easily see that in a radiology report and do a panic-search for its meaning and treatment. It takes clinical acumen to pull together a patient's laboratory and radiology findings to determine the most appropriate course of treatment. It often cannot be accomplished by patients using these types of online resources.

Because high-deductible plans require out-of-pocket payment for doctor visits, people are not seeing their physicians regularly. As an alternative, they are turning to these unreliable methods to self-diagnose and treat illnesses that really need professional medical attention.

3. SURPRISE BILLS

If you recall, bundling services means a patient pays one price for the many different facets of a procedure. Unbundling is when all of these are separated out, causing additional payments for services related to a procedure.

Surprise bills come in because many specialists, such as radiologists, cardiologists, and aestheticians, will bill their services late in the year in hopes that the patient's deductible has been satisfied. If it has, then they can collect payment directly from the insurance company. If not, they must collect directly from the patient, which is generally more complicated and less likely to be successful. This results in those surprise bills, which inconveniently materialize during the leaner winter months.

The patient may not be fully aware of all of the surprises their bill contains either. We see this demonstrated with 3D mammography, an advancement designed to decrease the number of times women have to return for further studies. The 3D imaging costs are substantially higher than 2D mammography. Roughly half of women do not medically need this additional radiation or cost. Yet it is regularly prescribed as the go-to mammography method in the mainstream system. The only evidence that 3D mammography decreases callbacks and improves sensitivity of breast cancer detection is in dense breasts. Women with fatty breasts or scattered fibroglandular densities do not benefit from 3D mammography.

If we take the scenario a step further, let's assume a 3D mammography patient is found to have a nodule. Typically, this patient would be brought back for an ultrasound, which is sufficient to determine treatment options. Mainstream healthcare system protocols often also require a diagnostic mammogram be ordered as well. Unless they are performing spot images, this test is a repeat of the same mammogram.

The average patient is unaware of all of this, and, most likely, they will walk the path set out by the imaging center's protocol, never realizing the surprising additional costs and unnecessary radiation to which the patient may have been subjected.

It seems obvious that the three groups participating in mainstream healthcare interconnect. What impacts the doctor impacts the patient and the employer as well.

We need a health insurance system that breaks out of the mold that the mainstream healthcare system has strapped us in. We need a plan that aligns the incentives of the three participating groups using healthcare. Doctors must be able to promote healing and get paid fairly for their service and investment in time and dollars for advanced training. Employers must understand their options, take the lead, and properly convey affordable healthcare options. Patient-consumers need consistent care that they can afford. All of this is achievable within the employer-sponsored healthcare plan if they are restructured to align incentives.

BONUS PARTICIPANT TESTIMONIAL

Dr. Scott Cherry | Chief Medical Officer, *Axiom*

I originally started out in military medicine, so I didn't have to deal with the traditional health insurance that we see in the United States for quite a while. Over the past ten years, since I've been out of the military, I have had exposure to it, and the insurance system is somewhat confusing, to say the least. The doctors actually don't know what kind of bills their patients will get, especially regarding fees for pharmacy, radiology, and a host of other ancillary services.

As I got older, I became the patient, and the thought of an emergency or unscheduled surgery bill was a constant concern. Then, over the past few years, I learned about direct primary care (DPC) and direct-pay services. It's really been a personal game changer for me, as a consumer of healthcare. I have traditional health insurance, but it is quite hard to get a timely appointment. So I actually do have a DPC provider that I pay for out of pocket on a subscription basis. It's been very efficient, cost-wise as well as for quality of care. I can be seen very timely, the costs are transparent, and they're actually quite low.

I've also utilized direct radiology services, which has also been a game changer. I mean, we're talking half to maybe even one-fifth of the cost than utilizing my traditional plan. I'll probably never use my health insurance for radiology services again.

In my previous role, I managed primary care physicians, and I can clearly see that DPC doctors have a much improved work life because they're not beholden to the system. They are not required to see a certain number of patients per day, and they can spend as much time as they need to with each patient. The doctor wins because there's no middlemen necessary, and they don't need a large staff to process insurance claims. This results in better outcomes, which is rewarding for them, without having to endure financial penalties.

As for employers, when I started at Axiom, about five years ago, pretty quickly our CEO was very focused on the cost of health insurance and the value that our own employees were getting. So he opened my eyes to look at how to improve the value of health insurance. For the employer who provides the direct-pay, subscription-based health-care model, the financial pressure of healthcare is allevi-ated, and they can use their profits more efficiently. All the way around, the direct-pay model is a win-win-win.

We've mentioned the term "direct-pay" or "self-pay" healthcare a couple of times throughout this part of the book. This healthcare model is most successful when it is "primary care centric" healthcare. What does that really mean, though? Prepare yourself for great news as we show you exactly how to break the healthcare mold.

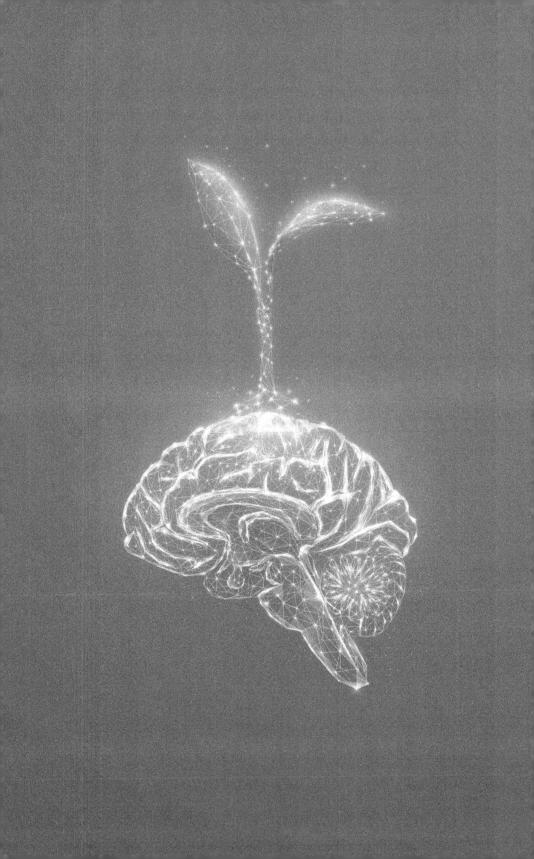

PART 3

Break the Healthcare Mold

Direct Primary Care

We spent some time discussing the limitations doctors in mainstream healthcare are under and what a typical primary care office visit might look like: fifteen minutes of consultation—for a patient the doctor hasn't seen in a year—which results in a referral cascade through the mainstream system for any new condition. Because the mainstream system boxes doctors into survival mode, instead of seeing a patient as a human being capable of robust health, the patient may be viewed more as a necessary sales transaction.

Some of us are old enough to remember a different way in which medicine was practiced. A general practitioner, or family doctor, was a skilled physician who diagnosed and treated ailments in the office or even in the patient's home. The current reincarnation of that doctor is the direct primary care (DPC) physician.

From a medical standpoint, roughly 90 percent of care can be administered right in the DPC doctor's exam room or by telehealth technology. Minor procedures, such as stitching up wounds, dealing with migraine relief, and treating muscle strains, are not referred up the chain; the DPC physician treats it.

Besides taking care of minor procedures and acute care issues, the DPC physician is focused on the patient's overall health and well-being. To accomplish this, they stay in regular communication with patients. Unlike many mainstream systems, the DPC physician personally sees and cares for patients. It's in the way they define "care," however, that the real difference is highlighted.

Whereas the average time mainstream-system physicians spend with their patients is fifteen minutes, the DPC physician spends about thirty minutes on that annual checkup, more if needed. If they are seeing a new patient, they often schedule a full hour to get to know the patient and their health goals, dig into the health history, and work up or address medical needs. They do not—in fact, most are adamantly opposed to—automatically turn to medications.

These doctors understand that proper diet, fresh air, and exercise create an atmosphere of health within the body. Did you know that the National Library of Medicine reports, "In general, our results support previous findings that physicians are not uniformly discussing weight status with their patients."?[36] In fact, studies show that doctors are receiving little to no education or training on this critical topic.[37] That is staggering when anyone who has even done a cursory study of the body systems knows that proper weight management is

---

36   Andrew C. Pool, Jennifer L. Kraschnewski, Lindsay A. Cover, Erik B. Lehman, Heather L. Stuckey, Kevin O. Hwang, Kathryn I. Pollak, Christopher N. Sciamanna, "The impact of physician weight discussion on weight loss in US adults," National Library of Medicine National Center for Biotechnology Information, accessed September 26, 2023, https://www.ncbi.nlm.nih.gov/pmc/articles/PMC4264677/.

37   Kimberly A. Gudzune, Veronica R. Johnson, Caroly T. Bramante, Fatima Cody Stanford, "Geographic availability of physicians certified by the American Board of Obesity," National Library of Medicine National Center of Biotechnology Information, accessed September 13, 2023, https://www.ncbi.nlm.nih.gov/pmc/articles/PMC6868336./

critical for overall health and well-being. The majority of healthcare issues could potentially be solved or prevented by implementing such positive lifestyle changes.

If we look at instances of fatty liver, for example, we see that if a patient were to lose ten pounds, their odds of becoming diabetic, along with all of the associated complications of the disease, reduce dramatically.

The body is designed to heal itself with proper nutrition. The DPC physician will focus on capturing chronic conditions and moving the patient toward nonprescription recovery. Diet and food choices become a healing force with this mindset. "Getting in shape" and "staying physically fit" are functioning medicines, not just positive lifestyle suggestions.

Similar to how a personal trainer meets with their trainee regularly to coach them on their workout progress, DPC physicians coach their patients on their health. Patients are seen regularly, and if the DPC doctor notices an issue, they will monitor it. They may ask how the patient did logging calories that week or note that a cold is lingering, possibly move that forward, and recommend a chest x-ray.

Does this mean the patient has to regularly block time out of their schedule to go see the doctor? Absolutely not. Most DPC physicians are strong proponents of medical technology advancements. They may recommend a blood pressure smartwatch, for instance, for remote monitoring of blood pressure. Heart rate monitors are similarly prescribed for patients who need this type of tracking. In addition, telehealth check-ins are used for the busy patient who cannot take time for consistent visits to the doctor. This model works in complete opposition to the appointment churn of the traditional, mainstream system.

One caution: Telehealth visits should be limited to supplemental check-ins when possible. They cannot fully replace regular, in-person visits with the DPC physician. One of the etiologies of recently decreased cancer diagnoses stems from a lack in pertinent tests being ordered for patients who predominantly use acute care telehealth. There tends to be a lack of incentive for the non-DPC telehealth doctor to order tests requiring follow-up. If they are ordered, complications often ensue regarding who will follow up on abnormal findings and to whom subsequent referrals will be made.

Subscription-Based Primary Care

DPC doctors' standard of care is impressive, but what's the catch? How are they able to perform all of this patient management, when primary care physicians in mainstream healthcare are stuck in the levels-of-care and referral system? Welcome to the healthcare model that is truly breaking the healthcare mold: subscription-based primary care.

The core difference that allows DPC doctors the freedom to practice medicine *with true care* is the method by which the DPC physician gets paid: patients subscribe to their services for a monthly fee; they do not pay for each encounter. This monthly fee grants the patient 24/7 access to their physician and may include 90 percent of needed care. How much is the typical cost? Between $50 and $200 per month, per individual, depending on age, market, and scope of practice and coverage.

Referring again to the Eastons, a functionally uninsured family with an asthmatic child, we saw that Mr. Easton paid $440 per month to his employer, directly through payroll, to carry his family's health insurance. In addition, they paid $3,000 per year, or about $250 per month, for their child's asthma supplies. A total of $690 is being paid out of their family budget for healthcare.

With a subscription-based DPC and health-sharing plan model, including unlimited access to their DPC physician for the entire family, they'd pay $440 per month. This includes a catastrophic agreement for emergency situations. The $250 they paid for their youngest's asthma supplies and medication could be reduced down to $0 because DPC doctors are able to find discounts based on income. Because of all of these positives, Mr. Easton would be able to cancel the policy through his employment, adding back $247 to their monthly finances. Their new budget for healthcare would look like this:

Beginning Monthly Healthcare Expenditures	−$690
New Sharing Agreement (includes coverage for any catastrophic event plus unlimited personal consultations with their DPC doctor for each family member)	−$443
Asthma medications	−$0
New Healthcare Budget Total:	**+$247**

We've clearly established that most patient-consumers are either already paying for their own health expenses or not getting the care they need. Yet the mention of paying their doctor a monthly subscription fee sometimes causes resistance. Patients have become accustomed to medical procedures billing in the tens of thousands, yet they're unsure about the value of a monthly commitment for health management.

The philosophy of the DPC physician includes guiding patients through the healthcare maze. They handle the business of healthcare, educate themselves on money-saving alternatives, and minister to the body, mind, soul, and spirit of their patients. Because they understand that the high cost of mainstream healthcare weighs heavily upon patients in all of these arenas, considering the patient's finances is part of their care/concern. Whether a patient is traditionally insured, creatively insured, or uninsured, the DPC physician acts as a healthcare Sherpa. They find resources and strategies to decrease out-of-pocket expenses for their patients and employers.

The Benefits of Working with a DPC Physician

t's important to understand what a subscription-based DPC physician is doing for the subscription dollars. Besides medical care that includes overall health and well-being, the DPC physician understands the healthcare system. They have the knowledge base and resources to work in—and around—that system. The advantages of this model are ever-evolving, but we have conservatively narrowed down eight of the top benefits of using subscription-based healthcare with a DPC physician:

Benefit 1: Pharmaceuticals

DPC physicians will do whatever they can to assist their patient on their healthcare path. When lifestyle changes can propel their patient to optimum health, that's the course of care they will recommend. If that's not quite enough and their patient needs medication, they are fully prepared to prescribe it, but they'll find the least expensive way of putting that medication into their patient's hands, especially very expensive medicines.

Part of the total-care, concierge service they offer is understanding the pharmaceutical industry. When we take a hard look, we see again that costs for medications—even common medications—are outrageously inflated in the mainstream system. Pharmacy benefits managers emerge as an unneeded middleman whose presence in the industry serves to inflate overall costs:

> Pharmacy Benefit Manager (PBM) Defined: PBMs are third-party administrators contracted by health plans, large employers, unions, and government entities to manage prescription drug benefits programs. They were created in the 1960s to process claims for insurance companies. By the 1970s, PBMs were serving as fiscal intermediaries adjudicating prescription drug claims. Today, PBMs not only adjudicate claims but also develop and manage pharmacy networks, determine drug formularies, set co-pays, and set criteria for prior authorizations and the patient's choice of pharmacy.

> Originally intended to process claims on behalf of clients within a set fee structure, they are often called "invisible middleman" because they are hidden between the patient's insurance company, who the PBM works for, and the pharmacy, who the PBM reimburses for dispensing the prescription. Currently the three largest PBMs, CVS Caremark, Express Scripts and OptumRx (a division of UnitedHealth-

care), hold nearly 80 percent of the prescription benefits market in the U.S.[38]

The DPC physician does not engage the PBM. Instead, they take on the real tasks of overall health management, including locating necessary medications and getting them directly into the hands of their patients. There are myriad resources DPC doctors can tap for accomplishing this that you'll never hear about in mainstream healthcare.

Benefit 2: Shopping

Shopping for health services is a labor-intensive, largely thankless task. Green Imaging has won several awards for world-class concierge service, and I can tell you, it takes full-time staff to find the best prices on imaging, outpatient testing, and other medical services. In the same way that they know the industry and how to locate the best pharmaceuticals, DPC doctors find patients affordable labs, testing, specialist services, and bundled surgeries. They look for, and network with, largely independent centers for their patients when possible.

It takes locating independent medical providers who eliminate unnecessary middlemen to get great care at an affordable price. DPC physicians are prepared to shop for and network with providers who can get their patients the best medical result for the least money out of pocket.

---

38   Pharmacists Society of the State of New York, Inc., "PBM basics," accessed September 13, 2023, https://www.pssny.org/page/PBMBasics.

Benefit 3: Virtual Consults

Virtual check-in with patients via telehealth monitoring is one aspect of DPC physician care. Another is virtually consulting with other medical professionals on the patient's behalf.

Let's say a patient presents with a broken finger. If you recall, 90 percent of care is taking place right in the DPC physician's office, so the situation will be resolved then and there. As the DPC doctor examines the finger and reviews x-ray results, she sees something that might require surgery and would like a second opinion. She would manage this by actually contacting an orthopedist by virtual consult, and together, they would determine the best course of care.

The orthopedist can review the situation virtually, hear the DPC doctor's concerns, and speak directly to the doctor and patient regarding any needed intervention or potential complications. If the finger just needs a splint, the DPC physician can manage that before the patient leaves the office. If intervention or further imaging is necessary, the patient will proceed with that course of care.

Benefit 4: Avoiding the ER

Once again, a trip to the ER can take small medical problems and turn them into mountainous bills. Conversely, regular medical attention and monitoring of minor conditions can keep most ER patients from ever getting to that critical level. DPC doctors understand this, and it is an intentional goal of theirs to keep their patients out of the ER. When both doctor and patient share this same goal and work together, the patient typically thrives.

If a patient ends up in the hospital system, say with a diabetic episode, the DPC physician will stay involved, consulting with the

ER doctor, providing information such as recent test results and prior diagnoses. They make sure lab results or imaging exams get into the ER doctors' hands to avoid redundant care. All of this is saving the patient time, providing a quicker, better analysis, and maintaining the best financial path forward (mind, body, soul, spirit, and financial care).

So if Mr. Everly has a diabetic episode and lands in the ER on Friday afternoon, his DPC physician will make contact with the ER staff, report any symptoms or indicators that may have led up to this, and if there is a history of severe episodes, they can alert the treating physician to previous successful treatment.

Benefit 5: Personalized Medical Care

Because the DPC doctor sees patients regularly, either in person or virtually, they are able to provide a personalized standard of care. When doctors hold patients accountable with genuine concern for their well-being, it makes a big difference in responsiveness to recommendations. If a patient knows they have a virtual well-consult on Monday, and their doctor regularly asks about diet and exercise progress, they tend to make better decisions all week long.

This model boasts regular evidence of sustained, long-term good health in the patients who use it. When people feel safe, or at least that they matter versus serving as a business transaction, *true* care for their health can take place.

Weekly, monthly, or quarterly interactions with a qualified physician can also reveal some of the deeper scars, such as abuse. If a patient continually presents with this bruise or that scar, their DPC physician, who truly cares, will recognize it. If abuse is taking place, they can help the patient through this trauma. Likewise, if there are indications of mental and/or emotional abuse or instability, the patient can be led toward appropriate treatment and action.

Benefit 6: Utilizing Specialists in a Modern Way

In the direct-pay model, with a regular DPC doctor tending to the majority of the patient's needs, what happens when that patient needs a specialist?

If a patient needs a specialist, such as a gastroenterologist, radiologist, or neurologist, their DPC doctor is going to find the most economical way to get the patient excellent care. As specialists treat patients, they typically fall into one of three categories.

1. SPECIALISTS SEEN EPISODICALLY

If you take a bad fall and break a bone, an orthopedist will x-ray the area. If surgery is not needed, they would follow up once to assure healing.

Likewise, if someone is rushed to the ER with appendicitis, a surgeon would operate on them once and follow up once to assure all went well.

A young adult with a sinus infection might require an otolaryngologist, better known as an ear, nose, and throat (ENT) doctor twice. The doctor will see them one time for an initial consultation regarding the problem, and once more for the follow-up.

In all of these cases, the doctor and patient may never see each other again, unless further care is needed at a later date. Total-care service includes shopping for the best doctors for these types of episodic conditions. DPC doctors will negotiate with different facilities, and they typically have a knowledge base of high-quality specialists who will both price the episode fairly and accept their patients.

2. SPECIALISTS PATIENTS SEE TEMPORARILY

Specialists whom patients see only for a certain period of time might include a dermatologist who treats a patient for a rash. The dermatologist may check them a few times until the condition completely resolves, but once it's gone, they will no longer schedule them for care.

The same would be the case with bunion surgeries. The orthopedic surgeon will see the patient regularly for about a year if both feet need correction. Once both surgeries are complete and the patient is on the road to full recovery, there is no need to see them any longer.

The DPC physician, again, will find these specialists and negotiate, frequently creating a bundle (all-in pricing) so that patients are able to get excellent care and hold down cost throughout the duration of their treatment (mind, body, soul, spirit, and financial care).

3. RECURRING SPECIALISTS

In the case of recurring specialists, the DPC physician can lead patients through truly innovative and cost-effective options. The same principle of subscription-based care can apply to recurring specialists.

In the case of Mr. Everly, our patient who was rushed to the ER with a diabetic episode, if his DPC doctor connected him with a subscription-based endocrinologist, what would be different?

If Mr. Everly regularly paid his endocrinologist a $75 monthly fee, he'd have 24/7 access to personal care. He'd have regular in-person and virtual office visits with this specialist. If he was feeling unwell at any time, he had access to personalized endocrinological care as well as input from his regular DPC doctor.

Likely, in this scenario, he never would have ended up in critical care. If he did, his care would have been enhanced and expedited by his endocrinologist's communication with the ER staff, and Mr.

Everly would have left the episode with as little out-of-pocket expense as possible.

Admittedly, the trick to utilizing specialists in a modern way is finding independent specialists willing to take on this style of patient care. They are out there, and the base of available doctors is ever-growing. The DPC physician will be fully aware of the regional market and will be able to guide their patient toward the right total care for them.

Benefit 7: Bundled Pricing

The subscription-based, direct-pay health coverage world runs on simplified price structures, and bundling prices for in-office or specialty medicine is the norm. The DPC doctor will, again, help the patient manage this, or they will manage it for them. They will advocate for bundled pricing for procedures, such as imaging and surgeries; they will endeavor to use outpatient surgical centers where they are more likely to get a fair bundled price for their patient rather than using hospital-system operating rooms where they often refuse negotiations.

If Mr. Jennings, for instance, needs surgery on his hand, the surgical facility must be booked; the anesthesiologist's bill must be considered, along with the surgeon's; and then there will be post-operative physical therapy and x-rays, which often get forgotten. All of these items must go into a proper bundling calculation. Mr. Jennings' DPC physician knows this and will advocate for the most comprehensive bundled packages.

Benefit 8: Better Care and Value for the Elderly and Veterans

Ultimately, the things we're talking about would be ideal for the elderly and our veterans. Let's take a condensed look at these benefits with an eye on these two vulnerable patient groups:

- a low-cost, subscription-pay plan

- the benefit of regular health management by a DPC physician who will get to know them, take note of any decline, and monitor their progress

- assistance with locating and obtaining needed medications at drastically discounted prices, if not for free

- a special eye on any mental health, depression, or abusive situations

- a doctor who takes time to care and apply their medical knowledge to keep them healthy in mind, body, soul, spirit, and financially

The elderly and our veterans are prime examples of those who do better—even thrive—when they are respected and treated with caring attitudes, regular interaction/checkups with their doctor, and being held accountable in a way that shows them their value. This model should absolutely be a part of government-sponsored healthcare, especially for those with chronic health conditions.

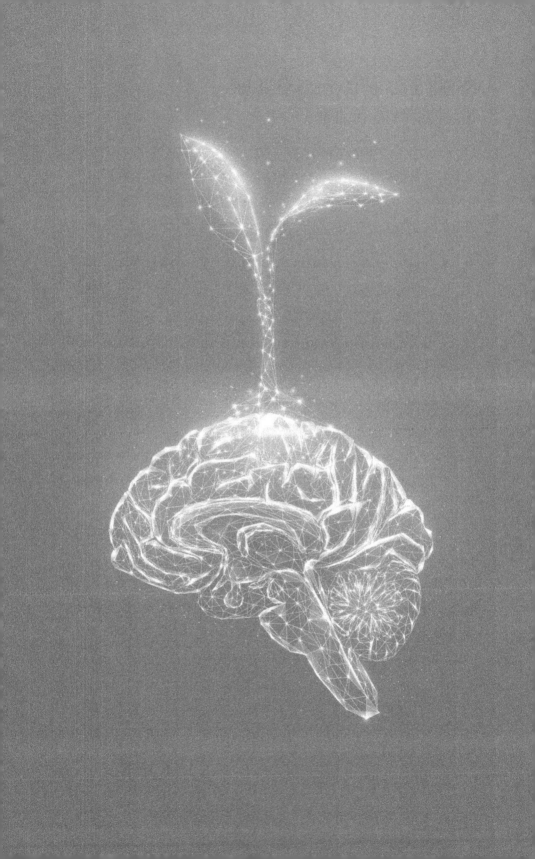

CHAPTER 12

Effective Catastrophic Care for the Direct-Pay Healthcare Model

I f you've come this far in the book, you may be feeling like one piece of breaking the healthcare mold is unclear, especially for those of us who self-insure: With all of the insurance options out there, how can you know the best one for your specific circumstances? What is the best way to insure singles and families alike against catastrophes?

You'll absolutely want to consult with your benefits advisor for expert advice in this area. However, for the purposes of providing doctors, employers, and patients with a health coverage example that, in my experience, best meets the requirements of the whole plan, we'll focus on one: health sharing.

Most members who understand the overall direct-pay health-care model gravitate toward a health-sharing plan. Companies like Sedera and Zion HealthShare understand the value of DPC and offer discounts for catastrophic care when a DPC doctor is engaged. These plans work with unshared minimums, which resemble deductibles but are typically manageable—around $500 to $2,500, depending on the plan you select. The amounts are nothing like the high deductibles of traditional mainstream insurance, where deductibles can reach $10,000 per calendar year. Once the unshared amount is paid, "health-sharing" or sharing costs with other members kicks in for a given health issue.

As an example, my husband recently needed shoulder surgery. Of course, he saw our subscription-based DPC doctor, and we shopped as many direct-pay facilities as we could. Then, we paid cash for the MRI, some necessary pre-op testing, and for the consultation with the surgeon. By this time, our $1,500 shared minimum had been satisfied, and the shoulder surgery was covered completely.

Here are a couple of examples of plans with catastrophic coverage, plus unlimited subscription-based primary care. Three factors will impact pricing: age, initial unshared amount, and group versus individual enrollment.

Family Coverage
Age: 30–49
Zion HealthShare IUA $2,500 + Unlimited Next Level Prime
Group family monthly: $443

Family Coverage
Age: 30–49
Zion HealthShare IUA $1,000 + Unlimited Next Level Prime
Group family monthly: $543

Sedera also provides this chart, which demonstrates the savings that are possible with their health-sharing plan:[39]

INDIVIDUAL: HEALTH INSURANCE VERSUS MEDICAL COST SHARING		
Health Insurance—$5,000 Deductible		Medical Cost Sharing—$500 IUA
Copay + RX $60	Dr. Visit 1	$100 Appt + RX
Copay + Shot $135	Dr. Visit 2	$150 Appt + Shot
Copay + RX $60	Dr. Visit 3	$100 Appt + RX
Copay + Shot $135	Dr. Visit 4	$150 Appt + Shot
Copay $35	Specialist	SHARED
$2,100	Surgery	SHARED
$2,525	Patient out-of-pocket + Annual Costs	$500
$21,000		$8,500
$22,525	Total	$9,000

---

39   Sedera, "Individual: Health Insurance vs Medical Cost Sharing," accessed September 13, 2023, https://sedera.com.

If you notice, this can work very much like the traditional model most of us are already used to using:

- The primary care doctor prescribes a test or procedure.

- Some out-of-pocket funds are necessary to reach your uncovered minimum.

- Once that uncovered minimum is met, as long as the patient-consumer continues to pay their premium, all remaining health treatment *for that specific health issue* will be covered at $0 out of pocket.

The only difference with the health-sharing model is that you will see direct-pay physicians throughout your treatment, as guided by your DPC doctor. These cash payments are typically much lower than mainstream insurance rates, and you will likely find the care to be outstanding. Although there may be a time of adjustment, there is nothing to feel overwhelmed or anxious about.

The Best Part about a Health-Sharing Plan

Here is the best part—and the reason those with understanding, and without significant preexisting conditions, often end up with a health-sharing plan: If you recall from chapter 1, we explained that a truly uninsured person who enters a medical facility for care and requests self-pay will be charged a self-pay rate, which very often can be a low multiplier of Medicare rates. If the person is insured, their rates are assessed via the contract with their insurance and chargemaster rates. This can run into many thousands of dollars more, depending on the procedure.

There's almost no way around this high cost. As soon as a few pieces of the patient's PHI are exposed, a scrubber "finds" their insurance status. Immediately, their chargemaster rates will apply unless the member is well educated on how to fight this using HIPAA Omnibus rights.

With a health-sharing plan, however, if a covered individual is in a catastrophic situation, their health-sharing insurance method is not recognized. The scrubbers will not find health-sharing patients as insured, even though their expenses will be "shared" and paid, above the unshared minimum. In this case, they may automatically qualify for the cash-pay rates.

The beauty of health-sharing plans is they provide a safe, familiar method for automatically qualifying for the lowest cash-pay rates available while still retaining the security of having quality, responsive health coverage.

Qualifying for a Health-Sharing Plan

One caution to note: With a health-sharing plan, there are usually health requirements for participation. Patients who have preexisting conditions may not qualify for all needed care. Some of the companies serving the direct-pay community, such as Sedera, are expanding those policies.

Smokers, for instance, who customarily did not qualify for health-sharing, now have options, although pricing is higher to match the health risk. For preexisting conditions, these companies are adopting policies that are allowing increasing coverage over a period of time.

Some potential members feel it's unfair to restrict participation in a health-sharing plan over lifestyle choices. The other members using the health-sharing plan, however, appreciate the low-risk pool that keeps their costs down.

BONUS PARTICIPANT TESTIMONIAL

Mike Walls | Experienced Direct-Pay Consumer

I've spent the past fifteen years coloring outside the lines in healthcare, and it just so happened that when we got pregnant with our third child, we were without insurance. We were scrambling, I won't lie, trying to figure out how to get a good doctor and hospital care throughout this time. The OBGYN was easy; we explained our circumstances and asked him what the cash-pay price for visits would be. He told us it would be $50. We were surprised because it was so affordable—and we were relieved because we could manage that price.

The hospital was a different story. When my son was born, he aspirated and was struggling to breathe. He spent six days in the NICU. Thankfully, he was all right, but we got a huge bill from the hospital—I think it was $75,000 or something insane like that.

Now, I actually owned a debt-settlement company at one time, so I have a little bit of knowledge about how to settle unsecured debt, but I'd never tried it with a hospital. At that time, I didn't know *I could* negotiate medical costs with a hospital. Then I thought, *Other services are negotiable; why not medical services?*

So I basically called the hospital and said, "You're charging me $75,000 for my son's birth, and I don't have insurance. There's absolutely no way I'm gonna pay this; what kind of options do you have available?"

We went through all the normal conversation with the discharge planner, as far as how they'll collect money. After a few weeks and some back and forth, it came down to me saying, "At the end of the day, I could pay you nothing, or I can write you a check right now for $6,000. We can handle it over the phone, right now, if you'll send me something that says you'll accept this as payment-in-full."

And what do you know? They said, "Yes."

That was our "ah-ha" moment. We can find medical services, and we can work directly with facilities to drastically lower our costs.

Down the road, I was self-employed and owned multiple businesses, so we were in a position to buy health insurance. When I started looking at the numbers, I was like, *What's the point?* To get a bronze, junk package would cost me about $1,800 a month, and I'd have massive out-of-pocket copays. It was the worst healthcare package out there. I mean, $1,800 in savings—that's a mortgage payment or multiple car payments.

Fast-forward to about five years ago, my daughter had some reoccurring ear infections. We knew she had a small hole in her eardrum, so we went to our ENT. She treated my daughter with antibiotics, which had the opposite effect than we were hoping. The hole enlarged to 80 percent of her eardrum. There was really no other option but to do some type of skin graft surgery, called a tympanoplasty, to fix that eardrum.

I didn't have any form of insurance—no catastrophic, no medical cost-sharing plans, nothing—but I knew how this game worked. I was determined to get out ahead of this and find the best price beforehand. I started calling hospitals in Houston, and no one at any of these facilities could give me finite pricing. One surgery center estimated a $30,000 to $40,000 cost; another one suggested it would be more like $50,000. It was absurd.

Throughout my research for the best direct-pay medical prices, I found Free Market Medical Association. Their website led me to find the Surgery Center of Oklahoma. They looked promising, and I was prepared to pack my daughter up and take her all the way there to get her the best care for the best price.

Before that happened, as I continued searching Free Market Medical Association, I ran across Sean Kelley's company, Texas Medical Management (which was called Texas Free Market Surgery at the time). So I went on their website, typed in tympanoplasty, and it came up with a $5,000 flat fee. I knew I was in the right place. I continued, entering the additional surgery my daughter needed, an ossiculoplasty. It was only another $250 extra for that procedure.

My cost went from a possible $50,000 to $5,250, and that included initial consultation with the specialist and the surgeon, the surgical procedure, and—if I'm not mistaken— a follow-up visit. The only real expense I had was my own hotel room for one night because I had to travel to Austin, Texas, for the surgery.

Along the way, my wife developed some kidney stones and had to have surgical procedures to remove them. Learning from this childbirth experience, we started calling ahead. The outcomes were the same—huge bill, and then I would negotiate a settlement with them for pennies on the dollar.

In another instance, my wife needed a CT scan, and the specific scan our doctor recommended was about $2,000. Instead of just accepting that price, I shopped online and found a local imaging place—I believe it was Green Imaging—that did the same scan for about $120. That's a savings of $1,800, and I don't have to worry about any surprise billing after the fact.

In the meantime, I had two other children, and we had to provide all of the medical care they required: dentists, doctor visits, fevers, school-physical requirements, and so on. So we started talking to our doctors and saying, "Hey, what's your cash price for an office visit?" A lot of them were $50. That was my copay when I had big-name health insurance.

Simply by paying attention and realizing the power I have as a consumer, I've been able to save myself some real money over time.

I had a buddy reach out to me the other day who has insurance through his company. He said, "Mike, health insurance, is bankrupting me, man. I'm paying $1,700 a month now, and I can't continue to do this."

I said to him, "What's really affordable *and simple* is direct primary care. I, or any member of my family, can see our DPC doctor at a moment's notice. For my family of five, I pay around $200 a month, or $2,400 a year. I get my doctor's personal cell phone. We can even FaceTime each other."

He challenged with, "Sounds great, but what happens when it comes down to an ER visit or long-term disease, maybe something like cancer?"

I didn't miss a step. I replied, "My family now uses a service called Sedera. It's about $500 a month, and it covers all of our ER and big catastrophic needs. Before I go into an ER situation, I know that my out-of-pocket expense is limited to $2,500, and that really gives me peace of mind."

He responded, "But my wife loves her pediatrician."

I said, "If you're not ready to make a wholesale change right now, then just ask your doctor what the cost would be if you paid cash upfront instead of using insurance."

He called me back a couple of days later and said, "You're

not gonna believe this: I called the pediatrician. He says it's $50 an office visit."

I said, "What about strep or flu tests? And how about vaccinations?"

He's like, "It's ten bucks for each of those things. Worst-case scenario, we show up, kid's got strep, they do a strep test—ten bucks. You get a penicillin injection—ten bucks."

Then I said, "Did you ask about telehealth? Because how many times do you have a kid who gets an ear infection or something like that? You don't need to go see the doctor and sit there for two hours to get a script."

He says, "Yeah; they do telehealth visits right over the phone."

I smiled knowingly and replied, "Welcome to the world of affordable healthcare."

If you're ready to break the healthcare mold and take control of your health and healthcare costs, you may be wondering how to go about doing that. How does the doctor switch their practice over to this model? How does the employer move their employees into a DPC-centric mindset? And how does the patient even begin to put all of it together and start saving cold, hard dollars? In the next section of the book, we'll discuss exactly that. So let's move on to how these three entities work together to make subscription-based, self-pay healthcare such a resounding success for so many.

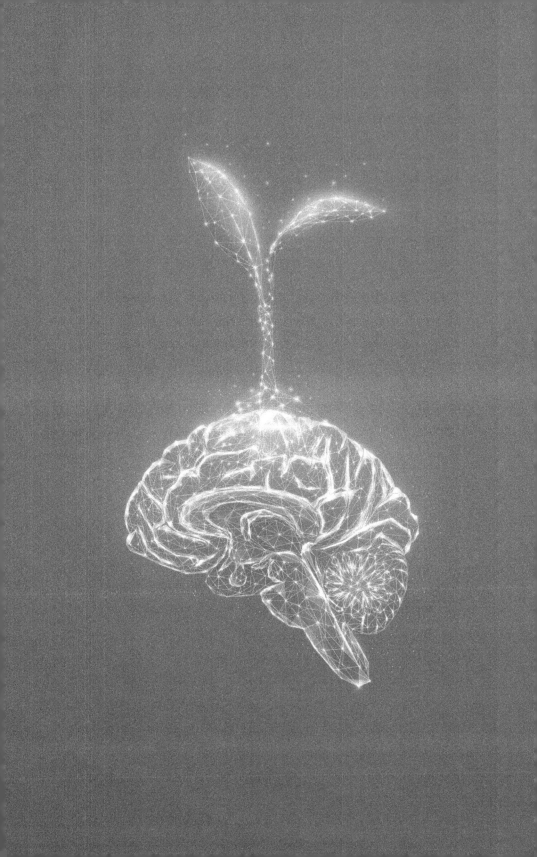

PART 4

How Physicians Break
the Healthcare Mold

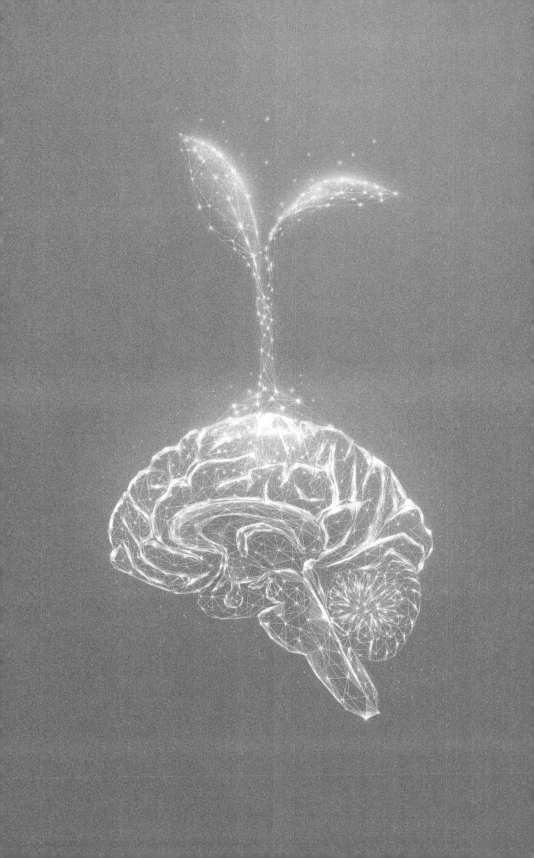

CHAPTER 13

PHYSICIANS—Direct Primary Care: Is It Right for You?

A friend of mine, Geetinder Goyal, MD, is a Yale-trained pulmonary intensivist. This brilliant physician switched course, altered his entire career, and became a DPC doctor. Why would he make such a drastic change? As an intensivist, he treated the critically ill in intensive care units. He saw patients with no end-of-life directive, so they had no control over the care they received. His observation was that the overwhelming majority of patients landing in his critical care unit never had to be there. Good primary care could have helped put them on paths toward better courses of care.

This stunning change in direction is happening for physicians of all focuses. They are realigning their practices to a direct-care model. They see that the quality of patient care is better, and the subscription-based payments provide a livable income. The question becomes, how do they do it? How do you, as a physician, make the switch to direct-care practice?

The best answer I can give you is to educate yourself about the DPC and direct-care communities. Take the learning process very seriously because there is a lot to learn. The specifics of how to establish a particular practice as direct care are as unique as each doctor and practice. New doctors just finishing up their residency will have different challenges than an established doctor with a full patient panel and staff to consider. A doctor practicing in a major city with direct-pay hospitals already open to contracts will have a different experience than the rural DPC doctor, whose options are limited. Here, I point you toward resources that can set you on your path.

Direct-pay coverage models excel in care and cost-effectiveness, but the ecosystem is still developing. Newcomers need information to move forward. Luckily, there are plenty of resources, helpful people, and ways to dip your foot or dive straight into the direct-care waters. I and many others are happy to mentor doctors, employers, and patients on their voyages.

Critics might say Green Imaging is just an aggregator pulling healthcare testing resources together. Not so. We consider Green Imaging to be a Direct Radiologist Care practice. I personally am a practicing radiologist, review patient orders to make sure the correct exam is performed, care about the patients, and interpret many of the exams. Our radiologists read more than half of the studies performed in our national network.

We encourage other specialists to think outside the box of the traditional pay model and create direct-pay practices. There are enough employers seeking alternative models for their health plans; there are certainly enough uninsured, functionally uninsured, and creatively insured patients lacking prompt and effective access to care in the traditional system to support a robust direct-pay community.

Locate and Connect with Established DPC Doctors

The best way to determine a path forward into direct-care medicine is to find doctors who are already successful in their practices. Most DPC physicians are more than happy to discuss their business and share resources with upcoming, interested doctors, both primary care and specialists. Many more conferences and websites on direct care are being developed. These platforms are designed to help direct-pay participants learn and network. If you're looking to sign on with an already-established practice, you'll likely find doctors in that capacity looking to hire.

Here are three conferences to attend for learning and applying the DPC model:

CONFERENCES

Direct Primary Care Summit

Whether you're just starting out or looking to expand the scope of your direct primary care (DPC) practice, you'll find the expertise you need to level up at DPC Summit. This is your opportunity to learn from nationally recognized faculty with years of real-world DPC experience. You'll find customized programming and hands-on workshops, plus you'll be able to:

- Network with other DPC enthusiasts who share your passion for whole-patient care.
- Discover the range of DPC options available in defining a DPC practice.
- Connect with expert vendors who offer the patient-centered solutions you need.[40]

---

40 "Direct primary care summit," accessed September 13, 2023, https://www.dpcsummit.org/home.html.

CONFERENCES

Docs 4 Patient Care Foundation DPC Nuts and Bolts Conference

Learn about the direct primary care practice model. Build a doctor's office free of insurance and other third parties challenging your clinical judgment and robbing your time with patients.[41]

The Hint Summit

Hint Summit is the direct primary care industry's premier innovation event of the year, bringing together direct primary care enthusiasts, pioneers, and innovators to share ideas, build meaningful new relationships, and celebrate the impact of DPC—all with the goal of growing the direct-care movement and making it the new standard in US healthcare.[42]

Doctors can find practical information, solutions, and assistance from many online resources. Some websites that exist to assist doctors with startup and continued success follow.

WEBSITES

Freedom Health Works

Your Trusted Partner for Starting a DPC Practice. We understand that starting a DPC practice can be challenging, and that's why we offer comprehensive support to physicians looking to transition to this model of care. Here are some reasons why you should let us help you start a DPC practice: Business support, marketing & patient acquisition, Technology & Infrastructure, supportive community. [43]

---

41   "Our 5th 'Nuts & Bolts to 2.0' Conference training hundreds of physicians in the Direct Primary Care practice model," Docs 4 Patient Care Foundation, accessed September 13, 2023, https://d4pcfoundation.com.

42   "The Direct Primary Care Innovation Conference," Hint.com, accessed September 13, 2023, https://summit.hint.com.

43   Freedom Healthworks, "The complete direct primary care solution," accessed September 13, 2023, https://freedomhealthworks.com/.

WEBSITES

Atlas MD

Poised to grow with you: Whether you're adding a doctor, or a new location, Atlas.md grows right along with you. Atlas supports inventory for multiple locations, doctor and patient location flexibility, and the ability to customize your practice how you see fit. Learn how to grow your practice, your way. Starting a direct-care practice or transitioning from a traditional clinic? We can help. Use our DPC Startup Kit to build your practice.[44]

Startup DPC

We are here to help you start and grow your direct primary care practice. Direct Primary Care is a dynamic practice model for delivering the best possible medical care to your patients and your community. Direct Primary Care allows you to be the doctor you were meant to be.[45]

---

44 Atlas MD, "You didn't go to medical school so you could fill out paperwork," accessed September 13, 2023, https://atlas.md.

45 STARTUP DPC, "How to start and grow your direct primary care practice," accessed September 13, 2023, startupdpc.com.

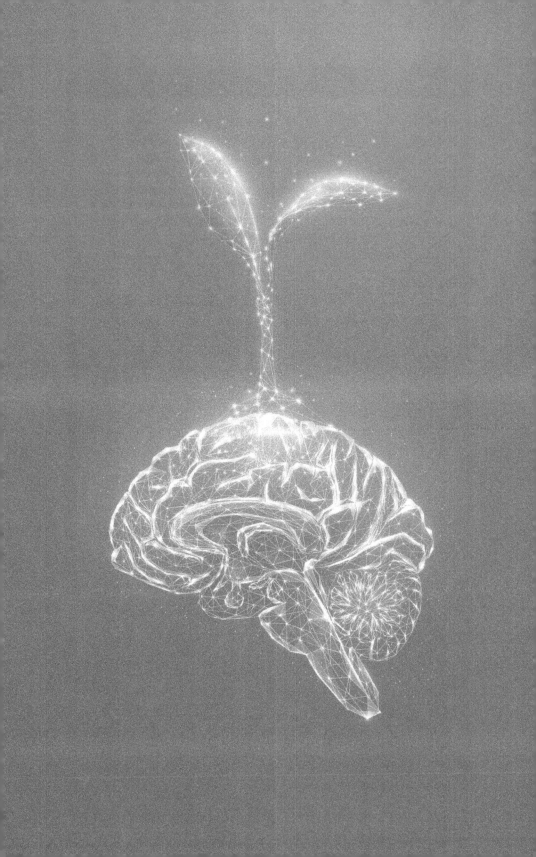

PHYSICIANS—Develop a Business Plan

W hether you're fresh out of your residency or an established doctor switching to a DPC practice, you will need to carefully create a business plan. There are, again, several excellent resources you can find online. Businesses like AtlasMD and Freedom Healthworks are dedicated to assisting DPC doctors, and assistance ranges from self-help to full management of your DPC practice.

Regardless of how much business management you intend to hire, these seven elements will be necessary to include in your business plan:

Perform an Honest Review

The initial business plan does not have to be overly complex, but you must do an honest, realistic review of your financials before moving forward. It's critical that you set a subscription price that works for you. To do that, you must know your real bottom line.

If you will be implementing a hybrid model, meaning you'll be accepting insurance as well as subscriptions, you must determine how much you really get paid for a patient visit. How much money actually comes into your practice from insurance? Are you spending money submitting claims and collecting bad debt? How much? It's necessary to establish the net return on all care.

Expenses

Again, take a hard look at your office rent, necessary insurances, and overhead. Do you have legal or other professional fees? How about your student loan payments? Put together a comprehensive list of your business expenses on a monthly, quarterly, and annual basis. Be sure to consider all your expenses when estimating your net income.

For example, consider this chart, which lists many costs a doctor might claim. Talk to your accountant about these and any other expenses that apply to your specific situation.

Advertising	Insurance
Electric	Internet
EMR	Janitorial
Health Insurance	Legal Fees/Lawyer
Licensing and Dues	Licensing
Office Supplies	Retirement
Payroll	Software
Phone	Taxes
Practice Management	Utilities
Rent	Vaccines

Your Pace

Most DPC doctors work with a patient panel of five hundred to one thousand patients. DPC doctors who contract with an employer may take on several hundred patients within the scope of that contract. As you can imagine, having one thousand *sick* patients would be difficult to impossible to handle. However, your goal as a DPC doctor is to keep your patients healthy. The healthier you keep them, the less they must use your services.

Just as the traditional system incentivizes doctors to keep bringing the patient back through the referral system, the DPC doctor is incentivized to keep the patient healthy and out of the office. They perform longer introductory examinations, get to know their patients, set up any remote monitoring that may be needed, and employ telehealth. DPC doctors typically do not need to see their patients more than once per year for a physical and necessary bloodwork.

As far as how many patients to schedule per day, 1 percent is the accepted industry recommendation.

To set your pace, determine your desired number of patients, and then do the math. If you are charging each patient $75 per month, five hundred patients will yield an income of $37,500 per month, six hundred patients will yield $45,000 a month, and so on.

Additional Education

Of course, you'll want to consider whether any additional education is necessary for you to practice in your state. For instance, I am a radiologist who has completed an internship. This meets the requirement for practicing primary care medicine in my state.

Not all medical licenses will qualify. Take the time to find out if you'll need any additional education before making changes to your practice. If you do, make a realistic, sound plan to obtain that education once you're certain you want to move in the direction of DPC.

Your Professional Services

It will be necessary, of course, to locate an experienced attorney to guide you through the legalities of starting your practice. For this endeavor, it really is best to use an attorney who is specifically experienced in handling DPC legal issues.

Your accountant or tax preparer will also need to fully comprehend and educate you about the unique tax structures pertaining to DPC services. Again, try to find someone experienced in the DPC field.

As a resource, DPC Frontier offers these types of legal and accounting information (dpcfrontier.com).

Your Team

The team you surround yourself with can make or break your success. Each phase of growing a direct-pay practice will rely heavily on team members who are flexible, pleasant, and have problem-solving expertise.

I have been amazed at how many of the companies with whom we work are family businesses. I believe the buy-in and trust a family business offers bring competitive advantages. If you are not lucky enough to have family members to fill trusted positions, make sure your personal ethics, work ethic, and goals are well aligned with your key team members and that you enjoy each other's company.

Marketing Your Services

Once DPC doctors have decided how big they'd like their panel to be, it's time to find patients. Doctors must involve themselves in professional relationships with DPC mentors, attend the conferences and meetings, and possibly stretch beyond their typical comfort zone.

When marketing, concentrate on the benefits of the direct-care model and what it can do for the patient and employer. Emphasize the cost savings as compared to mainstream care and the quality of care being offered. In some cities, such as Houston, DPC doctors have joined together and created a joint website where potential patients can find them. To move forward and make your services known, educate yourself and begin to network.

WEBSITES WHERE DOCTORS CAN ADVERTISE THEIR SERVICES	
DPC Frontier	dpcfrontier.com
Free Market Medical Association	fmma.org
DPC Spot	dpcspot.com/todo/marketing
FindMyDoctor.com	https://www.findmydirectdoctor.com/dpc/dim

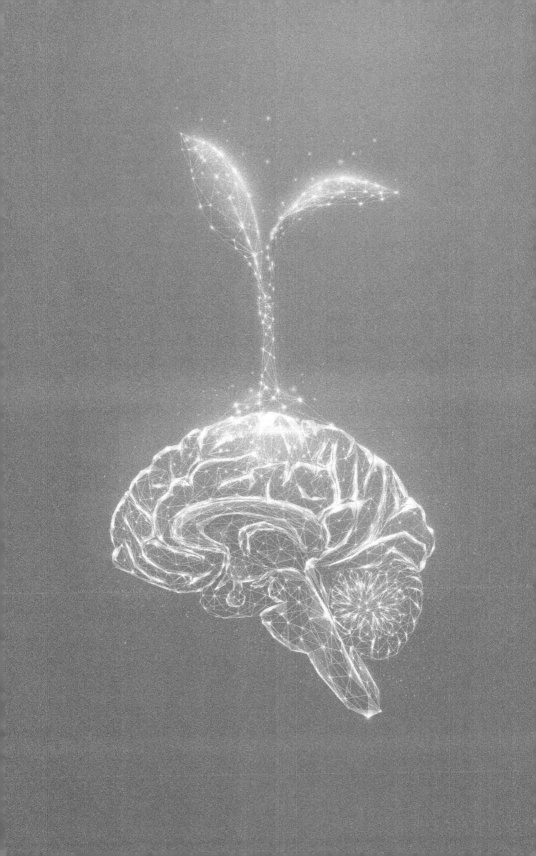

CHAPTER 15

PHYSICIANS—Startup and Maintenance of a DPC Business

The startup and maintenance of a DPC practice entail several parts, and the process has unique considerations for doctors. Will you run your practice using a hybrid model? What role do you as the doctor really play? How will you get your patients to retain your services when you make the switch? What about those pesky noncompetes?

Let's go ahead and start the discussion of startup and maintenance of your DPC practice right there, with noncompete agreements. Before any other business plans take place, and certainly before any financial risk occurs, you'll need to know if you can practice business in your locale at all.

Noncompete Agreements

As we've previously discussed, the noncompete agreements doctors sign in the mainstream hospital systems are often egregious and overreaching. Before setting out to change your practice in any way, be very aware of any noncompete agreements. Are you bound by one? What exactly are the terms?

Doctors starting out in their DPC businesses usually don't have difficulty getting out of their insurance contracts. The difficulty comes from dealing with years of inability to practice because of prior practice noncompetes, which can severely hinder your plan forward or be expensive to shed.

Hybrid Models

Many established doctors setting out to change their practice to DPC will begin that journey by continuing to accept mainstream insurances. Typically, this is a way to transition while doctors build their panel. Eventually, most move exclusively into the subscription-pay model. After all, they are making this move into DPC because of the flaws in mainstream traditional insurance.

Green Imaging is a prime example of this: we were originally established as a direct-pay imaging network. When the ACA was passed, there was great hope for better healthcare and more timely payment. So we participated in the program, thereby shifting us into the traditional insurance system. We quickly found ourselves in the same mainstream rut that we'd seen before in the traditional system: we were spending 30 percent of our revenue to collect 70 percent of what we were contracted to receive. We opted out of a $1 million revenue stream in 2017 to return to a pure direct-care model.

Deciding to part ways with insurance companies or Medicare becomes not only a financial decision but also one of conscience for many doctors. They have worked to care for their patients, and they built trust and rapport with them. Losing patients because they have traditional insurance seems as wrong as losing them because they do not. Each doctor will have to determine how to handle this dilemma. Many make the cold turkey cut, and others keep some insurance contracts while simultaneously practicing DPC medicine.

That said, individual insurance contracts will clearly state how to cancel. When opting out, it's important to find the termination requirements for each contract. They will vary from contract to contract, and termination must be followed precisely.

Onboarding Patients

Part of the DPC doctor's business plan must include onboarding patients in order to keep the practice flowing smoothly. An established primary care doctor onboarding their patients has an advantage, in that the patient already knows and has selected the doctor for primary care. On the other hand, doctors changing to DPC will have to accept some patient loss.

To minimize this, it is recommended that you start discussing what DPC medicine is with each eligible patient at least three months prior to your changeover. Enthusiastically point out the positives: longer appointment times, personal attention, 24/7 access to care, and, of course, the customary fiscal savings.

When the time comes to make the switch, simpler is better. Most DPC doctors will set up subscription portals right on their website with the necessary legal components included as part of the application for care. One tip I can offer from experience is to keep your conversion/subscription form to one page that explains the process and enrolls the patient directly.

Understanding the DPC Role

No matter where you come from in the medical community or how you want to establish your practice, there are certain expectations of a doctor practicing DPC medicine. If you recall, one of the benefits of using a DPC doctor is the role of Sherpa that they serve. It is key to their brand of service .

The very first part of your new Sherpa role will be guiding your patients on the way DPC works. For instance, patients may need to adjust to using video and/or text messaging to convey health concerns, or they may need instruction on how—and why—to use your contracted pharmacy.

By also guarding your patients' financial health, your responsibilities expand. When we get the middlemen of medicine out of the way, healthcare gets a lot easier—and saves the patient cold, hard dollars.

CHAPTER 16

PHYSICIANS—Direct-Pay Contracts and How to Apply Them

L et's take a moment to discuss what a direct-pay contract is and how they work. Doctors, employers, and patients will all need to understand what direct contracts are, how to use them, why it's necessary, and what it means to have a direct contract with a facility.

Direct-Pay Contracts

A direct contract occurs between a group needing medical services (patients, third-party administrators, employers) and the doctor or medical facility providing service. Prices are negotiated so that anyone within that contract can receive treatment at that facility for this reduced pricing as opposed to chargemaster rates. Contracted rates are agreed on between the group or the doctor and the medical facility, and they may be negotiated at a percentage of Medicare (reference-based pricing; RBP) or as a flat fee for services.

Be aware that Medicare rates differ by state and region, by whether the site of care is in an office or facility, and by Medicare status of the provider. Be specific as to which state, region, and status of Medicare participation are used for the fee schedule to which the contract refers.

Engaging the Direct Contract

The office manager, contract manager, or marketer in a medical facility is frequently the person who can help a group engage a direct contract. As incentive to the facility to accept your direct contract, be clear in negotiations that no insurance verification and preauthorization will be required, that they will receive prompt payment for services, and that the goal of the contract is to ensure zero patient bad debt.

Remember, half of the value equation is quality, so vet the facility and physicians as best you can, and continuously monitor patient satisfaction and outcomes. Beware of direct-to-consumer and direct-to-employer platforms that offer pre-negotiated prices; many of these have no quality guarantees or assurances.

Direct Contracting Combined with the DPC Physician's Network

A good DPC doctor has a network that optimally includes as many of the following six medical services as are available in the community:

1. direct lab services

2. direct radiology services

3. access to pharmaceuticals (even when opting out of CMS, maintain your Provider Enrollment, Chain, and Ownership System (PECOS) number for ordering and prescribing status)

4. options for catastrophic coverage

5. safe harbor hospital

6. access to direct-pay specialists

Let's take a look at each of these services, keeping our focus on the direct-pay contract and how the DPC doctor integrates these contracts with exceptional care for their patients.

Direct Labs

Direct lab service is usually the easiest to incorporate into a DPC plan. Quest Labs, for one, is generally open to direct-pay contracts, and they are located all over the United States.

Let's say DPC physician Dr. Mel creates a direct contract with Quest Labs for bloodwork panels at a flat fee of $30. Every one of the doctor's participating patients would be able to have a blood panel performed at that lab for this fee. By comparison, that blood draw might cost over $200 in the mainstream health system.

Direct Radiology

Direct radiology works in a similar way. Doctors or employers contract directly with the imaging facility, and participating members of those groups are able to receive substantial discounts when they use these contracted facilities.

Green Imaging currently contracts with radiology centers all over the nation. We buy unused time on their tables at a discount, send our patients to those local facilities, and then we read the study and report the finding, passing our savings on to the patient or employer. Think Travelocity: you buy from their website, but you're going to stay at the Marriott and enjoy all of their amenities.

DPC doctors make themselves aware of direct-pay imaging centers, customarily saving individual patients and employer health plans literally thousands of dollars.

Access to Pharmaceuticals

For standard medications, the easiest and most effective way to save is to simply shop for prices at various local pharmacies. The same drug may cost substantially less from CVS to Walgreens to grocery-store pharmacies.

It's necessary to shop for each medication a patient needs because so much price variability exists between each drug. For instance, Mrs. Barker, a sixty-three-year-old postal worker, needs both heart and cholesterol medications. When her DPC doctor prices her meds, the cholesterol drug may be found to be least expensive at a local grocery store, whereas the heart medication may come in substantially cheaper at Walgreens.

Generics, of course, are another way to save big dollars. The cash rates on some of these drugs are lower than copay rates. We figured that out ten years ago, when we were still insured with UnitedHealthcare. We had a $60 copay on a medication, but if we went with the generic version, the cash cost was only $10. We did not even have to involve our insurance at that price.

Sometimes the best recourse for the costliest courses of pharmaceutical treatment is using qualified medical facilities in other countries. Grand Cayman has a hospital system there that offers drug infusions at a fraction of the American cost. Sending patients to the Caymans for one weekend a month for their infusion treatments costs far less than it would to send them through the mainstream system; the savings are that pronounced.

DPC doctors are familiar with these methods of saving money on prescription medication. In addition, DPC physicians are aware of pharmaceutical trusts that offer drastically reduced prices on their medicines for eligible patients. Those who fall below 200 percent of the poverty line (27.5 percent of Americans)[46] can normally get these medications for free.

Considering patients who cannot tolerate certain medications, the DPC physician is free to apply their own strategies, such as prescribing only three days' worth of expensive medications, seeing how the patient handles it, and then filling the rest of the script if they do well on it. DPC doctors are free to practice medicine intelligently and prescribe pharmaceuticals with practical discretion.

Access to Direct-Pay Specialists

Specialists are needed and wanted in the direct-pay community. Their creativity and business sense may pioneer the next best practices in the

---

46   Lillian Kilduff, "How poverty in the United States is measured and why it matters," Population Reference Bureau, January 31, 2022, accessed September 13, 2023, https://www.prb.org/resources/how-poverty-in-the-united-states-is-measured-and-why-it-matters/#:~:text=In%202020%2C%2017.9%20million%20people,27.5%25%20of%20the%20population.

industry. DPC doctors keep up with these specialties and network to include their patients in specialty direct-pay care.

Dr. Kris Held, an ophthalmologist in San Antonio, is an outstanding example of specialty direct-pay service. She became so dissatisfied with trying to get eye surgeries approved through Medicare or mainstream insurance that she switched to direct-pay exclusively. Is her practice declining? Just the opposite; she's thriving. People choose the savings, accessibility, and the simplicity of just getting the procedure done.

Another specialist who is breaking the mold and offering cash rates is Dr. Huseng Vefali, an interventional cardiologist out of Austin. Without doubt, interventional cardiology at affordable rates can change the paradigm of higher-risk patients.

For ideas on drafting a business plan appropriate to their specialty, specialists can consult with others in Dr. Diana Girnita's Direct Specialty Alliance (https://dscalliance.org).

Safe Harbor Hospitals and Charity Policies

A safe harbor hospital is one with which a specific group, such as a DPC doctor or employer, has established a direct-pay contract. Rates for non-life-threatening services are contracted for pre-negotiated, direct rates, and historically, they are a fraction of the cost of mainstream chargemaster rates. Member-patients within this direct-pay contract who are seen at this facility pay for—or care is paid for on their behalf—based on a contract between the entity and the hospital.

Let's say fifty-three-year-old Mr. Wagner is a member of an employer group who is contracted with St. Joseph's Hospital. His employer has a pre-arranged, direct contract with this facility, and because their savings for hospital services at St. Joe's are so drastic, they are able to completely cover their employee's non-life-threatening visits to the hospital.

On his way home from work one evening, Mr. Wagner is side-swiped by an SUV, resulting in severe impact with the driver's door/window to his left shoulder. When the paramedics arrive, they know immediately that Mr. Wagner needs x-rays of the area.

Even though another mainstream hospital is very close to the scene, Mr. Wagner insists on going to the ER at St. Joseph's, which is twenty minutes away. Why? Because that is his safe harbor hospital, where he can receive treatment at contracted rates. Since his employer plan has a direct contract with St. Joseph's, it's possible he'll pay nothing out of pocket for his treatment at that specific hospital.

On the other hand, if Mr. Wagner allows emergency services to take him to any other hospital, he will be responsible for his treatment costs. If his employer supplements his direct-pay plan with traditional insurance for catastrophic situations, he will be subject to his copay and deductible should he use another hospital or emergency facility.

CHARITY POLICIES

Another avenue for hospital services that DPC doctors can explore is to appeal to a hospital's charity policy for discounts for their patient. Every not-for-profit hospital must have a charity policy. Usually, this policy provides either discounted or free care to patients who fall below a certain multiplier of the poverty line. In some localities, households making nearly $100,000 qualify for this benefit. So in the event that a doctor cannot connect patients to a safe harbor hospital and there is a hospitalization, the DPC doctor knows of methods that can assist the patient in getting costs reduced.

Options for Catastrophic Coverage

Most direct-pay health plans revolve around DPC care, and 90 percent of a patient's medical treatment will typically be handled in the DPC doctor's office for one, low monthly cost.

What happens, though, with the 10 percent of care that is not treated in the DPC office? That care must be paid for, either in cash through a direct contract with a safe harbor hospital or through some form of insurance.

The DPC doctor must be prepared to recommend best catastrophic options for the individuals and families whom they care for. This means they must not only have a knowledge of the field but also a network that includes benefits advisors to make this step as easy as possible for their patients.

BONUS PARTICIPANT TESTIMONIAL

Sean Kelley | Founder, Texas Medical Management

Before my brother and I developed Texas Medical Management, I had the opportunity to work inside the belly of a large hospital system, developing surgical practices in pediatric subspecialties with a focus on neurosciences. During that time, I learned a lot from surgeons and others about how to determine quality in surgical services. I also learned that there are many different ways to save money in surgery that don't impact quality in the least.

During the course of my time there, I came to see that the hospitals were disproportionately charging the patient, even for things that were relatively inexpensive in terms of hospital cost. So about seven years ago, I left that system. I knew that we could build something better: higher quality, better service, and lower cost.

My brother is a pediatric craniofacial and reconstructive surgeon. He has had the unique opportunity to operate collaboratively with surgeons all over Central Texas. From his experience, he created a list of the best surgeons in our area by specialty. When we decided to build a better system for surgery, we approached those surgeons and negotiated contracts with them, and that's how Texas Medical Management began. What we do is bundle episodes of care, mostly in the surgical space.

Almost everything in healthcare is episodic, meaning it has a distinct beginning and a very well-defined end. Most treatments are very specific, which means that they can be bundled together to make them simple to understand and easy to pay for, as opposed to this open-spigot approach that the traditional healthcare system seems to drive us toward.

We found independent facilities that were willing to negotiate fees with us. Our surgeons are interested in trying to drive down the cost because we pay them a lot more money than the insurance companies—two to five times as much—and they're paid within seven to ten days. They don't even have to send us a claim. They collect nothing from the patient because we negotiate contracts with no patient-out-of-pocket. I bring them all the medical records, all the different eligibility and authorization, so there's no worry about the financial aspects. It doesn't take very long for the staff to get onboard to the extent that we hear from the doctor, "Hey, could you send us some more?"

Then what we do is help them manage their costs. Today's facility fees include implants and sterile supplies, which often are 60–80 percent of the total cost of the case for the facility. We buy directly. There's no group purchasing organization (GPO) involved. We don't deal with insurance networks or others to negotiate contracts. We negotiate those directly, and we're directly responsible to the facilities and surgeons.

Seeing the results of this method for our patients has been the most rewarding part of our program. I could tell you hundreds of stories of how we helped somebody that didn't think they were going to be able to get care. Natalie is one of many examples. Natalie needed surgery, and when her father sought treatment for her, the surgical centers and hospitals quoted charges between $15,000 and $45,000. When he finally found us, we quoted him a total cost around $5,000. This made the procedure manageable for the family, and Natalie was able to have the surgery.

It is rare when an opportunity exists where you are able to create so many "wins" for the partners, patients, and their payer. The large health systems and their partners, the large insurance companies, are charging Americans so much more than medical treatment really costs. Even worse, they give us no information on quality and provide us with poor service, ranked second to last to cable companies.

In our model, we pay our peer-selected quality surgeons and other bundled providers better, faster, and with no cost to collect bad debt. Our patients get curated service and quality of care, and we do it by eliminating the middlemen who add no value to the patient.

As for employers, my business partner Joe and his family own L & F Distributors, the second-largest Anheuser-Busch beer distributor in the country. They have about 1,200 employees, and healthcare costs were an ever-growing, out-of-control expense. So they formed their own captive insurance company several years ago, and they've lowered their premiums and reduced their out-of-pocket deductibles multiple times by implementing a better quality of healthcare.

They started a disease-management program that has dramatically reduced hospitalizations. In today's workforce, we often see people in their twenties, thirties, and forties who are on blatantly unhealthy paths. This is where coaching comes in. The medical staff will sit them down, discuss better health strategies, and bring in a dietician to teach them about healthier meal choices and preparation. They help the employee-patient to understand nutrients and health benefits of foods and encourage healthy choices for the entire family, including cooking classes to help on a practical level.

Why would L & F Distributors, or any other company, go to such lengths? Because they know the cost of turnover. They know that the culture can never be built if it's constantly flipped on end with new people, and there's risk associated with that. So they spend an inordinate amount of time and money making sure their people are in good health because they want them to be there for decades. They understand that health coaching and individual attention from a caring physician—the foundation of DPC medicine—is the way to ensure longevity and quality of life.

No matter how you run your individual practice or what mindsets you adhere to, the direct-pay contract combined with the DPC doctor's network is foundational to the DPC doctor's brand of care. For instance, there are DPC doctors who run their practices with a purist mindset, meaning they believe the relationship between the doctor and patient is private, and no other entity should be involved. Others feel that, while this is a legitimate approach, contracting with an employer is what gets larger panels filled quickly and makes the DPC practice financially successful. Most DPC doctors are open to collaborating with employers to optimize patient coverage.

The three participants in healthcare coverage—the doctor, employer, and the patient—work together to make direct-pay healthcare flow. Each has their own responsibility to learn and apply the direct-pay method. Consider how the doctor and employer specifically support the whole patient in this model, as we move on to How the Employer Breaks the Healthcare Mold.

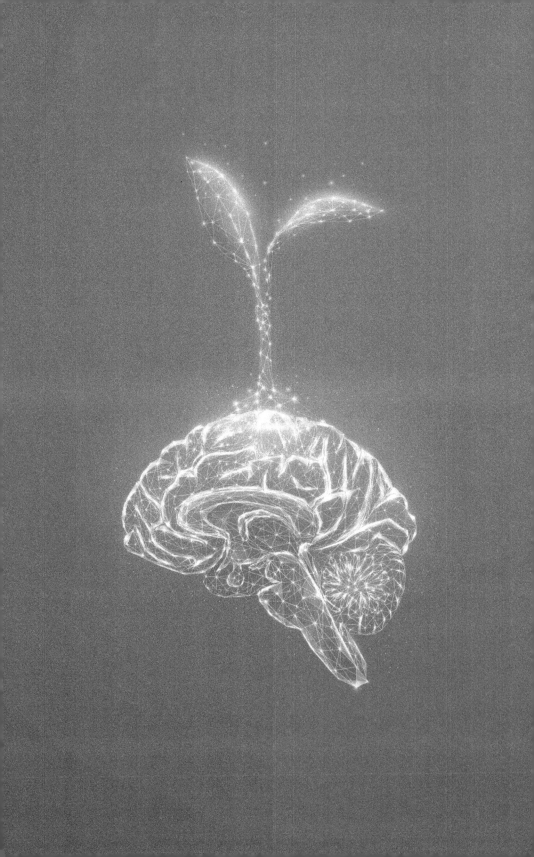

How the Employer Breaks the Healthcare Mold

EMPLOYERS—Nine Components of a Direct-Pay Health Plan

We took some time earlier in the book to identify the Death Spiral which occurred in the late 1980s through the early 1990s, wherein "employee costs to participate in the employer plan became too expensive; the healthiest employees began to drop off in favor of more affordable individual policies; [and] the remaining small employer risk pool was sicker, resulting in higher insurance premiums on renewal the following year."[47]

Harris Rosen, president and COO of Rosen Hotels & Resorts in Florida, was one of those employers who recognized that healthcare premiums were skyrocketing, and he made changes to control his costs and provide superior health services to his employees.

---

47   Gabrielle Smith, "The complete history of employer-provided health insurance," March 31, 2021, accessed September 13, 2023, https://www.peoplekeep.com/blog/the-complete-history-of-employer-provided-health-insurance.

Many on his team were immigrants with prior health conditions who had never seen a doctor before. The first thing they needed was regular primary care. Next, they needed instruction and resources to help them remain healthy. Yet these commonsense pieces to enduring health were completely ignored by Rosen's mainstream insurance company, while high-dollar procedures were quickly approved.

Instead of caving to the mainstream system when Blue Cross Blue Shield continued raising his healthcare premiums, Harris Rosen reinvented health coverage for his employees. In a bold move, he canceled his contract with Blue Cross Blue Shield and took on the responsibility of providing healthcare to his team. RosenCare, as his program is now called, is a resounding success and goes beyond traditional healthcare. Here are just a few of the life-changing aspects of Harris Rosen's healthcare plan:

- on-site medical centers on or near his properties;

- free transportation, during work hours, to receive regular medical care;

- health coaches and nurses;

- prioritized nutrition and cooking classes;

- robust on-site exercise classes such as kickboxing and Zumba;

- physicals, cancer screenings, and dietician visits;

- assistance with high-risk pregnancy/family planning and nursing.

Dave Chase reveals more about Rosen's astounding medical narrative of the times in his TED Talk, "Healthcare Stole the American Dream—Here's How We Take it Back":[48]

> One doctor in a large health system in California shared with me how he and his colleagues were getting pressure by the administrators to amputate diabetics' feet. You know why? Because it was taking them too much time to manage the diabetes.
>
> [With] Rosen, it's a different story. Employees who have diabetes work with a care team that have time to do what they do best, whether they are a doctor, a dietician, a health coach, a nurse, or a pharmacist: to reverse the symptoms of diabetes—and certainly never get to the point where they'd have to amputate.

As you might expect, this kind of care has helped Harris Rosen's employees to thrive. Mr. Chase goes on to note these two important statistics,[49] demonstrating that RosenCare worked on the whole person:

> Despite physically demanding jobs, on-site physical therapy has led to opioid prescription rates that are one-sixth of the national average.
>
> They have a mandatory stretching program for housekeepers and other employees with a higher risk of injury, reducing injuries by 25 percent.

---

48   Dave Chase, "Healthcare stole the American dream - here's how we take it back," TEDxSunValley, YouTube, accessed September 13, 2023, https://youtu.be/wKmbKEOUaQU.

49   Ibid.

RosenCare has become a pioneering model of direct-pay health-care to emulate, and Green Imaging is honored to have them as a client.

The Nine Components

Employers, you may not have the resources to do exactly what Harris Rosen did, but his innovation, resilience, and outright rebellion against mainstream healthcare protocol show us a path that is not only possible but has also been proven successful. You, as an employer, are *empowered* to take control of your bottom line while providing excellent health benefits to your team. Similar to your responsibilities when managing their 401(k), if your members are paying a significant percentage of cost out of pocket, you have a fiduciary duty to assure their healthcare dollars are well spent.

A fully implemented direct-pay health plan includes nine foundational components. You do not have to wait until all nine parts are contracted and ready to utilize before beginning to implement changes. In fact, it is often best to install just one adjustment at a time. The nine components of a direct-pay health plan are as follows:

1. Obtain a true benefits advisor with aligned incentives who benefits financially from the health plan's success rather than from higher costs.

2. Offer a subscription-based enhanced primary care solution.

3. Offer direct contract for medical imaging and testing.

4. Offer direct contract for endoscopy and colonoscopy and nonemergency surgeries.

5. Offer direct contract for lab and pathology services.

6. Find a transparent pharmacy solution.

7. Based on claims history, find solutions for needed chronic care.

8. Offer direct contract with a safe harbor hospital/emergency medical facility.

9. Assure appropriate catastrophic coverage for your health plan that discounts cost based on the above. Consider narrow networks, RBP, and innovative stop-loss companies as alternative to the Blue Shield, United, Cigna, or Aetna (BUCAs).

You may immediately notice that components two through nine, which mostly deal with patient care, were already discussed as responsibilities of the DPC physician. A good DPC doctor may be able to direct you in all of these areas. However, no employer, geographical location, or overall healthcare structure is the same. Things become a bit more complicated for employers who have long-distance employees. You may need to network a bit to meet all the healthcare needs for employees in different localities.

Let's take a closer look at these nine components and how you as the employer move your company to a direct-pay health plan.

Component 1: Obtain an Advisor

Not only do I recommend obtaining an advisor to assist you, but I also cannot imagine undertaking this journey without one. Like the DPC physician, it is critical that you study direct-pay healthcare and learn how employers implement the strategies. Very quickly, however, you may find yourself in the weeds. There are multiple avenues for employers to take, different healthcare rules apply based on company size, and every population and geography is different in how health-care is being delivered in that community.

The reality is that each employer must seek out and find how the direct-pay healthcare model fits into their company dynamics. Luckily, there are online communities where you can seek out answers, learn, network, and implement processes on your own. There are also full-blown third-party agencies that will guide you through each phase of transition so that your business and employees are minimally disrupted.

For information, products, guidance, and advisors to person-ally mentor you, these entities have proven excellence in assisting employers in the direct-pay healthcare space:

ORGANIZATIONS PROMOTING AFFORDABLE EMPLOYER-FUNDED HEALTH PLANS

Aspirational Health
aspirationalhealthcare.com

Only 25 percent of healthcare is in the control of the healthcare system. The other 75 percent is in the control of the individual.

Aspirational healthcare spends 75 percent of its focus on supporting the individual and the ownership/management of their own health.

Free Market Medical Association
fmma.org

The free market movement in healthcare is gaining steam. This is because of providers, patients, and self-funded employers, who believe that changing the way we purchase healthcare services is necessary, and seeking out value driven healthcare providers is important.

Our mission is to unite all of the islands of excellence in healthcare and accelerate the speed and growth of the free market healthcare revolution.

ORGANIZATIONS PROMOTING AFFORDABLE EMPLOYER-FUNDED HEALTH PLANS

Health Benefits Nation by Validation Institute
healthbenefitsnation.com

The premier event that convenes CHROs, CFOs, HR, benefits executives, and benefits advisors to break away from the status quo and accelerate the move to accountable, transparent, and high-quality employer healthcare.

Gain actionable insights from plenary discussions and focused track sessions including Whole-Person Health and Well-Being, Innovations in Self-Funding, and Benefits Adviser Leadership.

Health Rosetta
healthrosetta.org

We help public & private employers and unions provide better care for 157 million Americans while reducing health benefits spending by 20-40 percent.

Clarity: We simplify and illuminate the path to lower costs, better benefits, and improved outcomes.

Trust: We vet an ecosystem of people, products, services, and places that make change possible.

To begin immersing yourself in the direct-care community and learning the processes of direct-pay health programs, these books can be invaluable:

BOOKS	
Marshall Allen	*Never Pay the First Bill and Other Ways to Fight the Healthcare System and Win*
Dave Chase	*The COVID-19 Wake-Up Call, Relocalizing Health: The Future of Healthcare Is Local, Open, and Independent*

BOOKS	
Tony Dale	*The Cure For Healthcare: An Old-World Doctor's Prescription for the New World Health System*
Nelson L. Griswold	*Breaking through the Status Quo: How Innovative Companies Are Changing the Benefits Game to Help Their Employees and Boost Their Bottom Line*

Components 2–7: Cash-Pay—The Crux of the Plan

We have discussed direct contracts and how they are established. What is important to emphasize here is why paying cash up front for medical services creates a different market for healthcare.

In his talk as the keynote speaker at the National Alliance of Healthcare Purchaser Coalition 2022 Annual Forum, CEO of Orriant (Orriant.com), Darrell T. Moon, told a story of a time he downloaded the chargemaster for one of the largest hospitals in the state of Utah. The hospital's average overall gross charges on every one of its signed contracts averaged a 30 percent discount. The cash-pay discount, however, was 75 percent.

This means, as Darrell put it, "If I walk in and say, 'Bill me later,' I'm gonna pay for a liver transplant, $325,000 at that hospital. If I walk in with an insurance contract, the average price is $226,000. If I walk in with a credit card and put it on my card, it's gonna be $81,000."[50]

---

50   Darrell T. Moon, "How CEOs can fix healthcare for their employees, opening keynote presentation for the National Alliance of Healthcare Purchaser Coalition 2022 Annual Forum," accessed September 13, 2023, https://aspirationalhealthcare.com/keynote.

But this was just one hospital in one state. So Darrell decided to do the same for another larger hospital in Washington, DC—the very place the keynote happened to be held. At this hospital, the average contract discount was 39 percent, and the cash-pay discount was 60 percent.

Darrell said, "Organizations that have been doing this cash pay purchase of healthcare for years are paying less than 50 cents on a dollar for healthcare because they're simply paying up front. It's fundamental to completely transforming healthcare."[51]

Cash-pay, up front, is the crux of the plan. By way of an example from my own experience, before School District of Osceola County contracted with Green Imaging, its costs for radiology were staggering. After they direct-contracted with us, they saved $1.5 million in the first full year, $2.5 million in the second year, and $3.7 million in year three. Keep in mind, this was for diagnostic testing services *alone*, a fraction of overall healthcare cost.

51   Ibid.

CASE STUDY #1

THE SCHOOL DISTRICT OF OSCEOLA COUNTY · 1887

One of Florida's most financially challenged school districts.

CLIENT	Central Florida School District
COVERED LIVES	10,000
AREA	Suburban Florida
TIME PERIOD	January - December 2020

PROJECTED

	CIGNA	GI	% PER PROCEDURE SAVINGS	$ PER PROCEDURE SAVINGS
MRI	$ 1,415	$ 525	63%	$ 890
CT	$ 2,007	$ 388	81%	$ 1,619
US	$ 330	$ 250	24%	$ 80
X-RAY	$ 199	$ 100	50%	$ 99
Mammo	$ 300			

TOTAL ANNUAL SAVINGS (Projected): $1,322,860

ACTUAL

REALIZED SAVINGS: 61%

	CIGNA	GI	% PER PROCEDURE SAVINGS	$ PER PROCEDURE SAVINGS	# SCANS	TOTAL SAVINGS
MRI	$ 1,415	$ 467	67%	$ 947	248	$ 234,960
CT	$ 2,007	$ 420	79%	$ 1,587	167	$ 264,972
US	$ 330	$ 213	35%	$ 117	574	$ 66,969
X-RAY	$ 199	$ 86	57%	$ 112	205	$ 23,022
Mammo	$ 300	$ 227	24%	$ 73	328	$ 23,983

TOTAL ANNUAL SAVINGS (Actual): $1,523,294

TOTAL ANNUAL SAVINGS JAN - DECEMBER 2021: $2.5 MM

PROJECTED ANNUAL SAVINGS 2022: $3.5 MM

Analysis of Osceola School District 7K member/10K lives CIGNA spend vs. Green Imaging prices for same exams.
*Includes PET/CT, Bone Density, Mammogram and other exams not illustrated in Per Procedure snapshot tables.

One notable aspect of this report is the number of employees in Osceola County's group: ten thousand. Large groups have better chances of getting contracted, bundled rates for labs, imaging, and hospital and/or emergency services. Considering, once again, the business of medicine, this is logical. When one individual tries to contract with a hospital or emergency care facility, there is no leverage. Statistically, many hospitals and emergency facilities are reluctant, if not outright hostile, about negotiating with individual patients. Bring on the possibility of ten thousand local patients onto the scene, and things may radically change.

If your group is not large enough to motivate hospitals to embrace direct-pay contracting, consider networking with your contracted DPC physician. They are likely coming into the game with five hundred to one thousand patients, which carries more weight at the negotiating table.

Component 8: Safe Harbor Hospitals and On-site/Near-Site Clinics

The easiest way to steer your team to choose your direct-contract facilities is to engage an on-site or near-site safe harbor clinic. Many men—in particular, those whose jobs demand harsh physical tolerance, such as construction—tend not to go to the doctor. Having an on-site or near-site clinic makes it more likely that they will receive needed healthcare. Depending on the clinic, DPC and more emergent services may be available. If we return to Harris Rosen's strategy, he created on-site clinics near all of his company locations.

Interestingly, when our client School District of Osceola County (SDOC) redesigned their health plan, they realized that ER costs were one of their highest expenditures and that their high deductible and out-of-pocket max were making it difficult for members to access needed care. When Mr. Rosen heard about SDOC's dilemma, he offered his medical center to the health plan members as a near-site clinic, and a direct contract for health services was created.

This means that SDOC members can receive healthcare services from their health center at $0 out of pocket. Payment for those services will be made by SDOC at a contracted rate that is only a fraction of their previous cost for primary and more urgent care.

Today, many employers are pooling resources, and three or four employers may join forces to open a near-site clinic—another strategy designed to add leverage and hold down cost.

Component 9: Catastrophic Coverage

A decision you and your advisor will make early on is whether you are currently fully insured (buying insurance from a traditional insurer), or if your best move is to switch to a level-funded plan (where your company takes partial risk) or a self-funded plan (where your company takes a fully defined risk up to a defined catastrophic stop-loss coverage limit).

Part of engaging the direct-pay model—possibly one of the most important parts—will be finding the right catastrophic policy for you and your team.

Following is a list of different types of health insurance options for employers. We've already highlighted health-sharing plans, but for individual business reasons, another type of catastrophic coverage may be best for your company. I highly recommend retaining the services of an outstanding benefits advisor to help you select the right plan for you and your employees:

CATASTROPHIC COVERAGE OPTIONS

Level Funding	A level-funded plan combines the fully insured and self-funded plans. You make set payments to an insurance company or third-party per month, which creates a reserve fund for liabilities that arise. At the end of the contract, you may be refunded surplus payments.[52]
Self-Funded	A self-insured health plan (also known as a self-funded health plan) is coverage offered by an employer or association in which the employer (or association) takes on the risk involved with providing coverage, instead of purchasing coverage from an insurance company. What is the difference between self-insured coverage and fully insured coverage? Self-insured coverage means that the employer or association pays for enrollees' medical care directly. Fully insured coverage means that health insurance is being purchased from an insurance company (either by an employer or by an individual) and the insurance company will be the entity responsible for paying for medical care.[53]
Fully Insured	Health plans negotiate the price of medical services with certain doctors, hospitals, labs and other providers. That way, the plan, and you, pay a lower cost. These providers are in your plan's "network." If you visit providers who are not in your network, you may have to pay more.[54]

---

52 Rebecca Wilson, "Self-funded vs fully insured vs level funded plans," Blue Ridge Risk Partners, accessed September 13, 2023, https://www.blueridgeriskpartners.com/blog/eb-types-of-health-plans.

53 HealthInsurance.org, "What is a self-insured health plan?" accessed September 13, 2023, https://www.healthinsurance.org/glossary/self-insured-health-plan/.

54 Fair Health Consumer, "Choosing your healthcare provider," Narrow Networks, accessed September 13, 2023, https://www.fairhealthconsumer.org/insurance basics/healthcare/narrow-networks#:~:text=A%20narrow%20network%20simply%20describes,the%20insurer's%20online%20provider%20directory.

CATASTROPHIC COVERAGE OPTIONS	
Captive Policy	As a type of "self-insurance," captive insurance is a formal plan whereby a business owner forms his or her own bona fide insurance company to fund losses. There are many benefits of a captive insurance company. The insurance coverages are tailored to the needs of the business.[55]
Health-Sharing Plan	While traditional health insurance aims to pay for all healthcare needs, health share plans are designed to cover the basics and catastrophic care for people who are pretty healthy. But some health share plans are more comprehensive. You'll want to find out which programs fit your needs best as you compare companies.[56] This may be an option for smaller employers with younger, healthy employees. Employers may need to add a Minimal Essential Coverage option or Individual Coverage health reimbursement Arrangement (ICHRA) for compliance, and an advisor with specific experience with health shares is key to assuring compliance.

55   Capstone Associated, "Self-insurance," accessed September 13, 2023, https://www. capstoneassociated.com/captive-insurance/self-insurance/.

56   Ramsey Solutions, "What to know about health share plans," August 1, 2022, accessed September 13, 2023, https://www.ramseysolutions.com/insurance/ health-share-plans#:~:text=While%20traditional%20health%20insurance%20 aims,best%20as%20you%20compare%20companies.

EMPLOYERS—Startup and Maintenance of the Direct-Pay Health Plan

The way to save the most when installing a direct-pay health plan, frankly, is to completely opt out of the major insurances and utilize another option for catastrophic coverage. In some cases, however, this is not a practical choice, especially in the very beginning, when transitioning.

Hybrid Transitioning

Keeping the "security" of mainstream insurance intact while you show employees the advantages of direct-pay is a way to keep noise to a minimum. A hybrid transition can make changes easier for your workforce to understand and accept. You will likely want to address the learning curve required by continuing to educate and regularly incentivize members to follow through on their end. We consider this a pathway to $0 out-of-pocket health coverage. If members choose to use the mainstream coverage, they will be subjected to the out-of-pocket costs associated with it. If they use the DPC doctor and facilities with which you direct-contract, it is at $0 out of pocket.

Dr. Juliet Breeze found herself in that circumstance. She felt strongly that she needed to offer a traditional health plan for efficiently hiring strong nursing candidates for her urgent care facilities. Dr. Breeze knew that direct-pay would cover the majority of their health needs, so she pulled as much care as possible out of the traditional plan. Here are the highlights:

1. She contracts with a major network, but she also offers subscription-based primary care for her staff and their families.

2. Her Next Level Prime program manages primary care, urgent care, labs, and chronic conditions.

3. She contracts with Green Imaging for direct-pay radiology services.

4. She offers excellent pharmacy options and educates her staff on why they should avoid having prescriptions filled through their mainstream carrier.

5. She encourages her employees to use their mainstream network only in a true emergency/catastrophic situation. *This is the key to a hybrid plan working.*

If employers want to retain a mainstream network, even in the short term, this is an excellent hybrid example to follow. If you recall, mainstream health plan costs spike year after year simply because people use it. However, if group members do not use the mainstream health plan except when there are no other options, there will be few, if any, claims. *Without claims, your mainstream health plan costs remain relatively stable.*

Pace Yourself

Keep in mind, you are not required to wait any certain amount of time to implement changes. If your team responds well and you are ready to move to the next stage within a few months, go ahead and implement the next component. You can and should transition at your own pace. That said, a reasonable timetable for transition might look something like this:

YEAR 1	• Obtain an advisor! • Begin teaching employees about direct-pay and that, unless they plan to meet their deductible, they should be considered self-pay. • Begin exploring the best option to self-funding your health plan if you're not already doing so. • Contract for subscription-based primary care. • Begin exploring PBM/formulary changes for prescription drugs. Get your employees used to simple changes that are least disruptive to the current model.
YEAR 2	• Add direct contracting for radiology services, lab, and outpatient surgical services. By this point, employees have been initiated into the way this plan works. They should understand that using your direct-contracted facilities results in great care and costs them nothing. But it's possible that your imaging service is not in as many convenient locations as your lab service will be. Employee-patients may have to travel a bit to get to your contracted location. Add incentives for them to travel when needed.

YEARS 3+	· Add a direct-pay hospital/medical center to the plan.
	Conveying to your team that they must go to one specific hospital or emergency services center is often the most difficult part to get across. Why? Because when it's needed, the patient is obviously in distress. A family I know emphatically and repetitively taught their son to ask for a particular medical center in the event of an emergency. During his freshman year in college, away from home for the first time, he was in a minor car accident. Upset and needing care, where did he go? Straight to the nearest ER. By the time your direct contract with a hospital or medical center is put in place, be certain your staff is already familiar—trained if you will—to use the direct facilities with which you have contracted.

Including Your C-Suite

Most employers inherently know that their C-suite must be onboard to implement this level of change. Your chief human resources officer (CHRO), especially, will be invaluable in questioning the various dynamics, such as legal, financial, and practical barriers. HR is the first line of defense in any company; if there are disgruntled employees, they will hear about it. Your executive staff must understand the changes, why they are good for their own families and their coworkers, and be able to guide the whole team through a lengthy series of changes.

It's crucial that your C-suite believes that the reward for this endeavor is worth it. If they are dubious, there will be grumbling and complaining at the first learning curve—and there will be learning curves; you can count on it. You'll need positive attitudes, a willingness to learn and apply information, and an ability to work together as a team to revise and improve processes. When training your staff, be able to quickly have an answer, with logical reasoning, to these eight questions/concerns the C-suite specifically might need clarified:

Q: *If we, as a company, pay for 100 percent of our employee's labs, radiology, and hospital services, won't they be out of work excessively for appointments they don't even need?*

A: I'm a radiologist who has owned imaging centers throughout my twenty-seven-year career. I can tell you that, in those years, I've rarely had a patient seek imaging that wasn't needed and prescribed by their doctor. Patients do not take precious time off work and undergo unneeded testing. DPC doctors also report that patients generally respect their 24/7 availability.

Q: *If we contract with a DPC doctor as one of the first steps, we'll still have our high mainstream insurance premiums plus new monthly fees for the DPC doctor. We'll be paying even more every month for healthcare. Isn't this counterproductive?*

A: At first, it's hard for employers to see beyond this logic, because the DPC doctor is being paid for on top of their already outrageous PEPM (per employee, per month) health coverage. The savings down the line, however, average 20–50 percent. DPC is best considered an investment, and the DPC fees are startup costs. How fast you see your return on this investment depends on how incentivized employees are to use the DPC doctor and direct-pay services you engage. Typically, offices see that 70 percent of care that was going to hospital systems drops to 10–20 percent, and this greatly outweighs the initial and ongoing costs.

Q: *Traditional health insurance employer costs are 100 percent deductible. Does this plan have the same tax benefits?*

A: When properly constructed, yes.

Q: *What does "$0 out-of-pocket" for employees mean? How exactly will employees get all of this outstanding care without paying anything? Why are we, as employers, paying 100 percent of medical costs?*

A: Because mainstream healthcare premiums are so high, when employers change over to direct-pay healthcare, they see dramatic savings. When employee-patients stick to the plan and seek medical treatment at the facilities their employer has contracted with, the employer can afford to cover it completely and still achieve tremendous direct and indirect savings. Since the employer pays that far-lower cost directly, it is truly $0 out of pocket for the employees to utilize, yet the employer is typically thousands ahead.

Q: *How will we entice quality candidates and make the company attractive during the interview and hiring process?*

A: Having to explain an alternative healthcare plan to every potential employee, every time you interview, is an interesting problem. Since COVID, employers in our current economy face a lot of chaos and employee turnover. They need a way to attract and retain talent. The first thing candidates ask is, "What are the benefits?"

With a direct-pay plan, you could just say, "We have free healthcare." Wouldn't that both simplify things and make your company stand out in a positive light? Think of the recruiting power $0 out of pocket healthcare could provide.

Q: *How do we prepare our workforce for this change?*

A: Explain what a direct-pay contract means *for them*: $0 out-of-pocket healthcare, 100 percent covered; outstanding care from a DPC physician; greatly reduced pharmaceutical cost; personal attention for chronically ill patients; avoidance of the ER; and financial returns in the form of pay raises and/or bonuses. If you explain the reasons why you are making this change, and focus on how the plan benefits your employees, they have a much better chance of willingly grasping the details. Again, your advisor will be of indispensable value!

Q: *How do we deflect reactions that lead to negativity?*

A: When facing negativity regarding the changes, try to remain understanding. This type of change disrupts your employee's security, and it's not unusual for them to feel threatened. Incentivizing them to stick with the program will go a long way in affecting good attitudes. Try things like offering gas cards to reimburse them for longer drives, hold promotional lunches where employees can win prizes for knowing the most contracted facilities, or hold monthly drawings among those who have correctly utilized the plan. Offer lunch, time off, or another reward for its proper implementation. Keep things fun, educational, and positive as you incentivize your team to conquer any procedural learning curves.

Q: *How do we get every employee to use the contracted facilities?*

A: To really drive home the need for employees to follow your new healthcare directives, emphatically and repetitively teach, encourage, and reward your team for utilizing the doctors and facilities with whom you have contracted. It can't be emphasized enough that if they go to the facility you are contracted with, the cost will be $0 out of pocket for them. The local, well-known hospital may be closer, but the direct contract with your contracted facility allows the employer to completely cover the costs.

CHAPTER 19

EMPLOYERS—Foundations for Success

O f course, it's in the best interest of the employer to ensure that employees and their families have outstanding and convenient health coverage. The parent on staff who is concerned about a child's health will not be fully engaged in work life, and the employee needing chronic care may be repeatedly away from their desk because of the mainstream appointment churn. Clearly, the advanced technological monitoring and telehealth options that DPC doctors utilize make them wise choices for your workforce as a whole.

Looking to Harris Rosen's example once more, we note four concepts that were foundational to his success. Employers moving their teams into a direct-pay health plan would be wise to apply these four foundational attributes to their strategy.

Foundational Attribute 1: A Different Mindset

Harris Rosen's plan took guts, intelligence, creativity, and persistence. Frankly, for other employers to reduce their hemorrhaging healthcare costs, they must take on the same mentality. You must face a couple of questions head on: Are you frustrated and feeling "stuck" in a healthcare-cost spiral? If so, we're presenting solutions. How much do you want to save those dollars? You must be willing to forge ahead if the path gets unfamiliar.

Deborah Ault, president of Ault International Medical Management (AIMM), encourages employers to face healthcare decisions with these four questions in mind:[57]

1. What is your current per employee, per year (PEPY) cost, and what do you want it to be?

2. What is the noise level—the level of resistance—that you're able to tolerate in accomplishing that PEPY goal?

3. How quickly do you need to get to the target PEPY?

4. Is this new approach going to be something that you personally would benefit from, support, and enjoy?

I find number two to be especially relevant. Questions will abound, which is why obtaining an advisor to help you and your team move forward is the first component to our strategy. As I've mentioned, to make changes to a person's security is understandably alarming, and there may be distrust of a "new way" of obtaining healthcare. Not only is your mindset important but also that of your administrative staff,

---

57   Deborah Ault, "4 Critical questions to ask every health plan sponsor," ALM Benefits Pro, May 24, 2019, accessed September 13, 2023, https://www.benefitspro. com/2019/05/24/4-critical-questions-to-ask-every-health-plan-sponsor/?slret urn=20221020155957.

the families of the executives, and every employee—each with their own medical needs. Are they all willing to learn and participate? This is a circumstance in which educating them and giving them time to acclimate to the idea of the change will save you a lot of noise.

The employer mindset shift is that the company is empowered and able to do great things for its employees, which is actually quite freeing.

The mindset shift for the employee is that mainstream health insurance is doing virtually nothing for 75 percent of them. It's bleeding their workplace dry, preventing raises, and still costing them thousands in high deductibles and out-of-pocket expenses.

Don't be surprised if you need to push forward and be persistent with the learning process, both for yourself and for your employees. You should be creating health awareness in your workplace at this point. That mindset is the beginning of educating your team. When you make health a priority and show that you care about your team's well-being, employees tend to respond by also prioritizing their own health.

Foundational Attribute 2: Workplace Culture

From the RosenCare example, we see these three dynamics working together to create an exceptional workplace culture: promotion of physical health, emotional health, and providing support for the healthy lifestyle RosenCare encourages. Let's break that down and see how it applies to you and your business.

Promoting good physical health in your work environment may be unexpectedly challenging. Some employees are required to sit at computer stations eight-plus hours per day; others, conversely, perform harsh, physically demanding duties.

Employers can promote physical health by encouraging sedentary employees to take regular ten-minute powerwalks, exercise in the company gym, or provide gym memberships as part of the $0 out-of-pocket healthcare plan.

For those workers with physically strenuous jobs, consider adding preventative treatment options, such as massage and strength coaching, to your $0 out-of-pocket health services.

Investment in preventative health maintenance is likely to result in far less spending on major health issues and/or injuries down the road.

As for an emotionally healthy workplace, Stress.org reported the following troubling statistics in a press release: "The vast majority of American workers say they are stressed, more than a third say that their job is harming their physical or emotional well-being, 42 percent say job pressures are interfering with their family or personal lives, and half report more demanding workloads than they had a year ago."[58]

These statistics can—and should—be vastly improved upon with some workplace conscientiousness. Employers can start promoting an emotionally healthy work environment with some basic strategies. *Forbes* identifies ten ways to improve your mental health at work. Encourage your team to see themselves, their time at work, and their coworkers with these strategic attitudes:[59]

---

58   Harris Interactive, "Attitudes in the American workplace VII," Stress. org, accessed September 13, 2023, https://www.stress.org/wp-content/uploads/2011/08/2001Attitude-in-the-Workplace-Harris.pdf.

59   Caroline Castillon, "10 ways to improve your mental health at work," Forbes. com, May 8, 2022, accessed September 13, 2023, https://www.forbes.com/sites/carolinecastrillon/2022/05/08/10-ways-to-improve-your-mental-health-at-work/?sh=250b7b6fdbc6.

1.	Begin your day with mindfulness.	6.	Accept rather than judge feelings.
2.	Focus on your strengths.	7.	Get outdoors.
3.	Stop comparing yourself to others.	8.	Do things for others.
4.	Start a gratitude culture.	9.	Find the humor.
5.	Talk it out.	10.	Learn something new.

When it comes to actually providing that healthy workplace, you have to be intentional with your choices in your office and culture. For example, there are now interesting options in vending machines, with salads and other wholesome foods offered instead of candy and chips. Employers choosing such options for their employee common areas create the most automatic environment for healthy eating. Foods that are prepared and easy to obtain are the ones chosen, especially for busy employees. Providing healthy food selections—less fried food and bad fats, more vegetables—generally results in employees consuming these healthy foods.

Harris Rosen also provided a healthy workplace by sponsoring cooking classes, with nutritionists available to teach healthy meal prep. He arranged for necessary vaccines, family planning, regular exercise classes, and more without any cost to his employees.

Investing the money it takes to "provide health" may be understandably intimidating. Remind yourself of the hundreds of thousands of dollars in savings these programs typically generate. It is not wasteful spending when both your turnover and absentee rates drop dramatically.

Healthier employees will cost you far less than unhealthy ones!

Foundational Attribute 3: Rewarding the Team with Better Pay and Benefits

It's important for your team's morale to see the reward for complying with all of these changes. You likely promised them that the company would be saving thousands of dollars per year with this healthcare revolution. They need to see that savings coming back *to them* and/or their community for the most enthusiastic continued participation.

Harris Rosen exemplified this attitude as well, as explained in Dave Chase's *Healthcare Stole the American Dream*: "At Rosen, they know that investing in education is at the foundation of achieving the American dream. So they take money that would have otherwise been squandered in healthcare and they pay for college for their employees and their employees' children."[60]

No wonder employees for Rosen are overwhelmingly satisfied employees.

Employers, reinvesting your savings back into your employees is not only a noble thing to do, but it also creates the loyalty you want—exactly what's needed in such unstable economic times.

Foundational Attribute 4: Giving Back to the Community

The fourth foundational attribute is giving back to your community. This often-overlooked piece of the RosenCare success story is what really exemplifies a business's far-reaching success.

---

60   Dave Chase, "Healthcare stole the American dream - here's how we take it back," TEDxSunValley, YouTube, accessed September 13, 2023, https://youtu.be/wKmbKEOUaQU.

Mr. Chase, once again, explains RosenCare's theory of success around this issue in *The COVID-19 Wake-Up Call*:[61]

> [Rosen has] also used money that would have been overspent on healthcare to fuel a range of creative philanthropy. [He] started by paying for preschool in the underserved, once crime-ridden Tangelo Park neighborhood in Orlando. He has also continued to fund various programs to help those kids develop, such as paying for their college education in full (tuition, room/ board, and books). The results have been breathtaking:
>
> - Crime has been reduced by 78 percent.
>
> - High school graduation rates went from unacceptable to nearly 100 percent.
>
> - 77 percent of Tangelo students who go on to four-year schools complete their degrees, exceeding the national average.

These types of astounding accomplishments occur when businesses decide to give back to their communities. Whether it's a million-dollar investment or sponsorship of your local little league team, giving back to the community is often a foundational attribute to successful endeavors.

---

61 David Chase, The COVID-19 Wake-Up Call, Relocalizing Health: The Future of Healthcare is Local, Open, and Independent (Seattle: Health Rosetta Media, 2021), https://healthrosetta.org/friends/.

BONUS PARTICIPANT TESTIMONIAL

Dr. Karen Rakers
Chief Medical Officer, Next Level Health & Wellness

As the chief medical officer over the Prime Health and Wellness divisions of Next Level Medical, I oversee our Prime program as well as our on-site employee health clinics. The big picture is that the cost of healthcare in the United States is skyrocketing out of control, and we can't sustain this in the long term. It's particularly difficult for employers, who are the main purchasers of healthcare insurance plans for their employee groups. In order to control and save costs, many employers have switched over from a traditional, fully insured plan to self-funded or self-insured-type insurance plans.

At Next Level Medical, for example, we are self-funded. We write the check when one of our employees seeks healthcare. This gives employers more flexibility in their finances, and they can focus on making different choices than they did previously. Employers are trying to figure out ways to help control costs while still providing high-quality care.

To meet this need, we offer the Next Level Prime program as a membership. We contract with employers; the employer directly pays us for the services; and employees and their dependents have access to primary care, preventive care, chronic disease management, and urgent care services. We include common panels of lab tests that we can perform in our own central lab, routine vaccinations, health coaching services, and emotional wellness counseling in the membership, for a fixed fee. The direct-pay model cuts out the middleman, which is the insurance company.

For our regular urgent care patients, we still deal with insurance carriers, and it is an entirely different experience. We submit claims, and sometimes they are rejected. Then, we have to argue, make corrections, and resubmit to get paid for the services that we have already rendered to the patient. It's necessary to employ staff to handle these claims and make sure future claims are in compliance.

This is all administrative, backend detail that really has nothing to do with actually delivering care to the patient. It drives costs up significantly and causes a breakdown in the patient–physician relationship because we have this insurance entity in the middle of that relationship. No reps from that insurance company were in the exam room; no one talked to the treating physician; they were not involved in the conversation or care of the patient—yet they often dictate what medication can be prescribed, what tests can be ordered, and what treatment plan will be made available to the patient. It's literally a third party that has nothing to do with what's happening in the exam room, and they're telling the patient and the doctor what they can and can't do. It's not good practice for the doctor or the patient.

By comparison, our subscription-based model flows so much better. We really are giving people significantly increased access to medical care and trying to make it as convenient as possible. We have a virtual platform where patients can manage much of their care from home. We also offer in-person and virtual appointments during hours when most primary care offices are closed, such as seven o'clock in the evening on a Saturday. Patients need not take any time off of work to get the medical attention they need, and there are no out-of-pocket charges for the patient. The Prime membership includes these services, and it's already paid for through their employer. Participating employers, again, are paying significantly less than they would have to pay if they had gotten all the same services under their traditional insurance policy.

Why wouldn't someone get the care they need when it's made this easy and affordable? Our goal is to help patients stay healthy for a long time to come.

In closing this section, I want to remind us all again of the fiduciary duty an employer undertakes when handling healthcare. Employers who take this duty seriously and face it head on will recognize that traditional, mainstream insurance is not money well spent. Direct-pay health plans, on the other hand, have a record of success and large monetary savings.

Consider also that the emergence of a direct-pay ecosystem as an alternative to the traditional healthcare system is dependent on engaging a critical mass of patients and doctors engaged, and employer-funded direct-pay health plans are an accelerator of the growth needed to make it a viable alternative nationally.

Take the time to learn about this growing field and get involved in the direct-pay networks. Go to conferences like Free Market Medical Association; find outstanding consultants and benefits advisors who can connect you with the best solutions for your workforce. Create your own paradigm, employers, one step at a time.

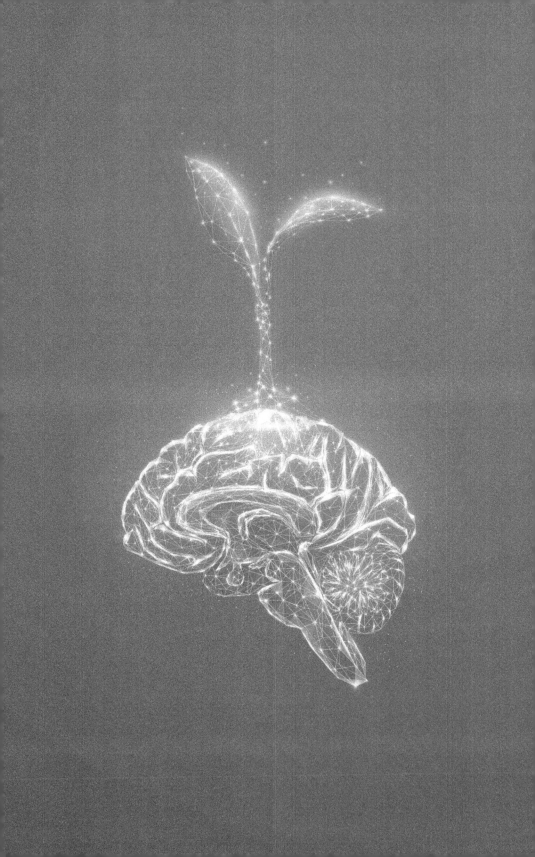

PART 6

How Employee-Patients Break the Healthcare Mold

CHAPTER 20

PATIENTS—The Business of Your Personal Healthcare

ndividual patient-consumers, you will be glad to know that your particular voyage to breaking the healthcare mold is much simpler than the doctor's or the employer's. That is not to say there will not be challenges. My husband and I have run the gamut of trying alternative insurance plans. Some do not meet the catastrophic threshold for many Americans. By applying the principles of direct-pay healthcare, we have saved well over $100,000 in this time frame despite absorbing most healthcare costs directly.

It's clear that for all three participants in healthcare, the savings are customarily outstanding in the direct-pay model, none more than the patient. However, this brings us to one very important question for individual patients: *Is the direct-pay method the right choice for everyone?*

Who Is Not a Good Candidate for Subscription-Based Care?

Patients with preexisting chronic illness who are at risk for stroke, cardiac events, and/or any complications will incur medical costs that are better covered with traditional insurance; some autoimmune diseases and transplant patients are also better off with traditional insurance models for catastrophic coverage. Why? The sheer cost of treatments, hospitalizations, and the advanced medical equipment needed to treat these illnesses will likely make the traditional system better in these situations.

These patients can still greatly benefit from adding DPC and subscription-based specialty care to their overall treatment. The regular monitoring and outstanding medical attention DPC doctors provide can be invaluable. Pharmacy, labs, and imaging costs can be controlled. Likely, the DPC physician will connect with specialists and involve themselves in the patient's whole treatment. As we mentioned, more and more specialty doctors are entering the direct-pay community. It's quite possible that the DPC physician can steer that high-care patient toward better treatment and improved cost-effectiveness, regardless of their traditional insurance status.

Direct-Pay without—or in Spite of—Your Employer

The vast majority of patient-consumers will obtain insurance through their employer. Oftentimes, they feel they must go along with whatever process their employer has set up, whether medically or financially beneficial to them or not. This is untrue! Just as the doctor and employer can use a hybrid method of traditional and direct-pay insurances for their purposes, so can you as a consumer. The following nine tips are relevant for any patient-consumer who wants to take control of their healthcare and have a money-saving health plan. For those of you who will manage a hybrid model in spite of your employer's healthcare provisions, these tips are especially for you:

1. USE THE EMPLOYER'S TRADITIONAL PLAN AS IF IT'S CATASTROPHIC ONLY

If you recall, Dr. Juliet Breeze with Next Level Urgent Care developed an effective employer hybrid model. Here is a brief summary:

1. She contracts with a major network, but she also offers subscription-based primary care for her staff and their families.

2. Her Next Level Prime program manages primary care, urgent care, labs, and chronic conditions.

3. She contracts with Green Imaging for direct-pay radiology services.

4. She offers excellent pharmacy options and educates her staff on why they should avoid having prescriptions filled through their mainstream carrier.

5. She encourages her employees to use their mainstream network only in a truly emergency/catastrophic situation. *This is the key to a hybrid plan working.*

As a consumer, you would duplicate this method by having a catastrophic policy in place; you would engage a DPC physician; you would use the labs, radiologists, and pharmacies that your DPC doctor recommends; and of course, you would use your catastrophic coverage only in the event of a true emergency or situation that your DPC doctor cannot treat in their office.

2. FIND AND ENGAGE YOUR OWN DPC DOCTOR

DPC doctors or specialists can be found using the many websites and resources designed to introduce you to the direct-pay community. If doctors are going to specific sites to market, it makes sense that you as a consumer go to the same sites to find them. Here is a refresher list of those resources:

WEBSITES	
Atlas MD	https://atlas.md
Freedom Health Works	https://freedomhealthworks.com
AAFP	https://www.aafp.org

ADDITIONAL WEBSITES FOR PATIENT-CONSUMERS	
DPC Frontier	dpcfrontier.com
Direct Primary Care Coalition	dpccare.org
Direct Specialty Care Alliance	https://dscalliance.org/

BOOKS	
Marshall Allen	*Never Pay the First Bill and Other Ways to Fight the Healthcare System and Win*
Dave Chase	*The COVID-19 Wake-Up Call, Relocalizing Health: The Future of Healthcare Is Local, Open, and Independent*

BOOKS	
Tony Dale	*The Cure For Healthcare: An Old-World Doctor's Prescription for the New World Health System*
Nelson L. Griswold	*Breaking through the Status Quo: How Innovative Companies Are Changing the Benefits Game to Help Their Employees and Boost Their Bottom Line*

3. FOLLOW THE PATH

Just like employers have to train their teams to use the direct-pay facilities they've contracted with, you will be listening in the same way to your DPC physician. Very simply, use the lab, imaging, and specialist services in your DPC doctor's network, paying cash for services.

Mr. Finn, a thirty-seven-year-old bodybuilder, refused to comprehend this. Within the first six months of retaining his DPC doctor, he was in the gym and felt a pop in the piriformis area that shot clear down to his knee. Making the injury all that much worse, he decided to "tough it out" and continue his strenuous workout routine. By the time he confessed his discomfort to his DPC doctor, imaging was needed to analyze the extent of the injury.

When his doctor recommended the imaging center she had contracted with for direct-pay rates, Mr. Finn scoffed. It was on the other side of the town, whereas the local hospital system had a popular center close to his home. He'd even been there once before, and he knew exactly how to traverse the grounds.

Waving off his DPC doctor's warnings, he went to the hospital system's imaging center. They took his Blue Cross Blue Shield card, smiled, and made everything easy.

When he received a bill in the mail for $2,800, because of his out-of-pocket responsibility, of course, he was stunned. His DPC doctor sat him down and explained again that had he gone to the imaging center on their contract, he'd have received the same outstanding care for less than $500. The light finally went on, and from that point onward, Mr. Finn listened carefully and followed the path his DPC doctor set out.

4. EMBRACE THE TELEHEALTH OPTION

The traditional healthcare system is notorious for functioning during weekday hours. Therefore, telehealth may be a more convenient option for patients with a full-time commitment to their daytime job.

When Miss Cooper was experiencing a skin rash on her left forearm, she was able to see her DPC physician the day her symptoms appeared. After applying the topical cream he prescribed, for $0 out-of-pocket, she was doing much better.

One week later, she was able to keep her follow-up appointment via a telehealth consult during her lunch break. This was an amazing convenience, as she had summer plans with her earned time off, and she didn't want to waste hours on doctor visits.

For many, telehealth is one of their first introductions into DPC medicine. Most often, they are thrilled with it, and they continue moving forward with expanded DPC services.

5. WHAT TO DO IF YOU'RE ADMITTED TO THE HOSPITAL

Al Lewis maintains an outstanding website for direct-pay healthcare called Quizzify.com. There, he explains[62] that ERs are required to treat anyone who seeks care there. Before they'll admit you to the ER, they'll typically first have you sign an electronic contract. Many people simply scroll, scroll, and scroll to the bottoms of these forms so that they can quickly sign their names and click submit. When you do this, however, you're actually agreeing to be responsible for any charges not covered by insurance—and if you're self-paying, that's all of them. What can you do to avoid this? There are four simple actions you can take:

1. Lewis advises that you insist on being provided a physical copy of the contract to sign instead.

2. Find the line item that says, "I understand I will be responsible for charges not covered by insurance."

3. Insert the word "reasonable" before "charges," and add, "with disputes to be settled by binding arbitration using the New York law as a model." *(That law is based on Major League Baseball binding arbitration rules, and it's well accepted. Using it has generally been a successful tactic for those who've needed it.)*

4. *Or* simply cross out the line altogether; they still have to treat you.

---

62   Al Lewis, "Six things employees should know about surprise medical bills," Quizzify, February 28, 2022, accessed September 13, 2023, https://www.quizzify.com/post/six-things-employees-should-know-about-surprise-medical-bills.

6. APPLY THE RULES INTENTIONALLY

Be creative and intentional in applying the rules of direct-pay. When you were stuck in the mainstream, if you needed to see a dermatologist, for instance, you might have called the one you drive by every day, or one that a close friend recommends.

Now, as a DPC patient, your first step toward treating that dermatological issue would be to consult with your DPC physician and see if they have a recommendation who will work with direct-pay patients. Again, it may not be the closest one, but you will be getting the very best value for your dollar.

> **Tip:** Companies like Sedera and Zion HealthShare have referral lists and are typically able to assist their members with finding an appropriate specialist.

7. PATIENT ADVOCACY

Patient advocacy is a service that is available to patients in some health plans, and a number of qualified nurses will work in this capacity with direct-pay patients.

Graith Care is a leader in the patient advocacy space, self-described as an independent patient advocate "[breaking] down healthcare barriers to save time and money while bringing back control and transparency to you as the consumer." Their services include providing "medical advocacy, consultation, advice, and recommendations in the US and internationally."[63]

---

63   Graith Care, accessed September 13, 2023, https://graithcare.vitafyhealth.com/gc.

Depending on how much care the patient requires, these nurses can meet with them if they are hospitalized and advocate for them throughout their hospital stay. The nurse may sit with a patient and monitor their condition; if the specialist is scheduled to see their patient at nine o'clock on Tuesday morning, they make sure that meeting takes place; if the doctor ordered IV fluids, they make sure said fluids were administered and that the bill is appropriate.

In many cases, this additional set of qualified eyes on a patient's care can not only be cost-effective but also lifesaving.

8. THE IMPORTANCE OF YOUR DPC PHYSICIAN

It's often best not to take coverage with companies dedicated to the direct-pay community, such as Sedera and Zion HealthShare, without the guidance of a DPC physician. A couple I know began using Sedera without a DPC doctor, and it was somewhat disruptive. The DPC community streamlines many health issues more efficiently; therefore, trying to mix the mainstream insurance appointment-churn mentality with that efficiency mindset created misunderstandings.

By comparison, in the second year that this couple used Sedera, they added a DPC doctor to their strategy. Their whole experience changed from lukewarm to positive. Your DPC physician knows how the parts of the direct-pay model work together in unison. Having them there to guide patients through the rough spots makes a critical difference in the plan's success.

9. HEALTH SPENDING ACCOUNTS AND HYBRID HEALTH MANAGEMENT

If your traditional employer-sponsored plan offers a Health Spending Account (HSA), you can truly create your own hybrid plan. Money set aside in an HSA account is tax deductible. With properly chosen contributions, you can pay for many direct-pay services with these designated, tax-free funds. Again, you are using your employer-sponsored traditional health plan for catastrophic needs only.

There is a warning involved with HSA card use: an HSA card comes in the form of a pre-loaded debit card, and it's sometimes too easy to use. I am suggesting that you spend very carefully; talk to an accountant about designating contributions and expenditures properly, and use HSA money to support your direct-pay plan.

What often happens is the convenience of having the card combines with the convenience of using nearby mainstream health facilities.

Something medically concerning is happening in your world at the time that this seems like a good idea. "Making things easy" is part of the psyche of a person in these circumstances. You must make diligent decisions to stay on plan and use the HSA card wisely and within the scope of your direct-pay plan. Once you start paying deductibles and "grabbing your prescriptions" with HSA funds, you are moving yourself back into the mainstream healthcare rut. Just like dieting, once you move off plan, it's very difficult to get back on track.

BONUS PARTICIPANT TESTIMONIAL

Laura Turcotte
Laura Turcotte Marketing Strategy & Design

We have health insurance, but we rarely use it. It's there for any catastrophic events. For our day-to-day healthcare, we go out of network and arrange direct, cash-pay rates with our providers: primary care, dental care, radiology or labs, any medical service that arises. It's worth it to us to negotiate directly with the medical provider.

I feel like the direct-pay model allows doctors to make more money, which allows them to slow down, which allows them to actually spend some time with us, as their patients.

I'm fifty-seven, and I finally found a primary care physician whom I love. She's outside of my health plan, which means I pay her cash. We spend actual time together; she knows about my life; she knows about my husband; she knows about my daughter; she knows about weird things that have happened to me physiologically. So she takes the opportunity to pull that all together when discussing my overall health.

Every other experience I've had going into a doctor's office, I mean, they're like robots—because they have to be. They've got to take notes and comply with certain rules. They're not even looking at me, the patient; they have so much documentation that all they're doing is looking at their iPad. They're focused on typing and getting all the right wording in, not on my health.

Transparent pricing is another huge benefit of this model. I'll never forget an experience I had when my daughter needed an MRI. Her doctor referred us right down the hall at the hospital—just like Dr. Dickerson always says. When we sat with the financial planner, she began with, "Well, your MRI will be about $1,800."

My husband and I are in the medical field, so we understand the subtle word games. I replied, "What do you mean 'about' $1,800? You have a negotiated rate with my health plan; you know the price Cigna will allow; we know how much I'm going to pay you today ... so tell me my costs."

She actually said this in response, as if it were a satisfactory explanation: "Well, that's really private information."

Astonished, I clarified, "It's my health plan; it's my health plan's contracted rate with you, but it's private information?"

Without hesitation, she said, "Yes; we can't disclose that."

Needless to say, we ended up going somewhere else, where we got a reasonable price. The traditional insurance roller coaster wasn't over with yet, though. The imaging center did not bundle the procedure, and we received an out-of-network bill from the radiologist. Of course, I questioned it; why would the radiologist be out of network? The reason is because that particular radiologist wasn't contracted with our insurance plan. However, no one explained this little detail or gave us a choice in radiologists.

About a month after that, one of my clients said, "Hey, I'm working with this doctor who's got this really cool healthcare model"—and I met Dr. Dickerson. She was solving the exact problem I'd just experienced. The reality is, if you were to study her data, it's true that she saves participating employers so much money that it's worth it for them to carve radiology services out and give it to their employees for $0 out-of-pocket. The direct-pay model is astonishing in its simplicity and effectiveness.

I'd like to encourage you, the patient, in the same way I encouraged the doctors and the employers: Take the time to get involved with the direct-pay community. Visit the websites, read the books, and go to the conferences. You will learn, grow, and meet others who can boost you onward and advise you in this healthcare journey.

The patient is the most important member of the direct-pay community. The difference in attention, respect, and care is reason enough to embrace this health coverage option. When you add the cost savings that the average DPC patient experiences, it stands out as a superior option for medical care for many Americans.

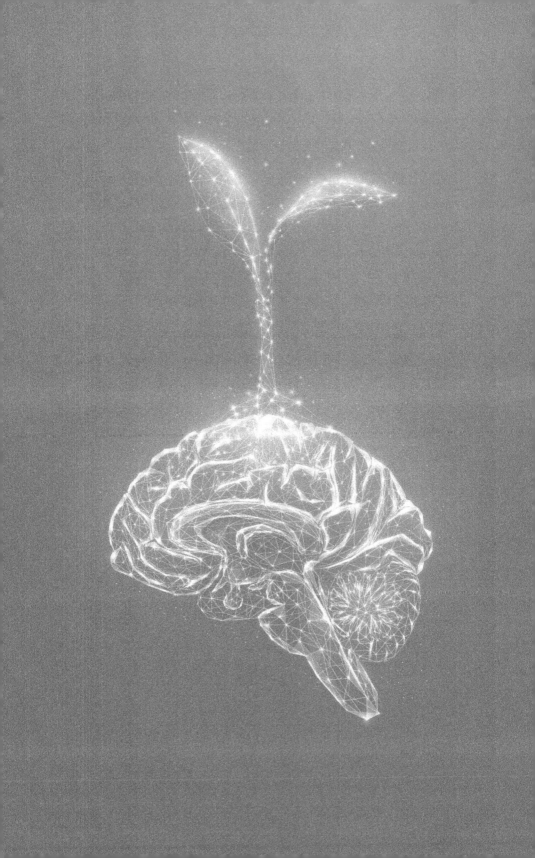

CONCLUSION

I t has truly been my pleasure to spend time conveying the benefits of direct-pay health coverage. It's my sincere hope that your voyage to free or greatly reduced cost healthcare has been simplified through this book. As I look at this developing community, I can't help but envision the future, and I hope for universal change to come. I soundly believe that the direct-pay model can, and should, replace the traditional system on a national scale.

Doctors

For the doctor, this future brings financial independence and freedom to fulfill your purpose, two ideals that are under attack in the traditional mainstream healthcare system.

When I was running a multispecialty clinic, we weathered a gap in Medicare payments that lasted two and a half months. It becomes nearly impossible to run a practice with this kind of financial delay, not to mention the staff who get diverted from their regular duties to handle such a situation. Upfront payment—better yet, regular subscriptions for services—eliminates doctors' dependency on mainstream insurance for their livelihood.

Ann Richardson, MBA, boldly discusses the "moral injury" to doctors that mainstream healthcare has brought upon them. On Episode 184 of *Primary Care Cures*,[64]

> I can save your life, but I get paid less for my work than some hairdressers.

What an eye-opening statement! Doctors in the mainstream system are regularly struggling financially.

When we talk about moral injury, we're talking about the emotional effect that these systems have on our doctors. They chose this career because they're passionate about helping people, but in practice, they're burned out because they're not given the resources— be it time, materials, staffing, and so on—to care for their patients in the way they deserve, and this weighs on them.

As a hospital administrator in the mainstream healthcare system, Ann shares that "[o]ver the years I was pretty punished and abused and silenced from the beginning because I was told I cared too much and so forth. So I'm on the outside now, and it's unlikely I'll ever go back *'on the inside,'* as I call it—because I feel like it's doing time."

As shocking and alarming as that statement is, Ann Richardson isn't alone. She explains that many doctors and nurses share her feeling of "doing time" when they're on mainstream health-system payrolls. The feeling is identified by a constant undercurrent of feeling like you're walking on eggshells.

---

64   Ron Barshop, "Episode # 184 – Ann Richardson is the DocWhisperer. She is letting the bigs know a frontline exodus is hitting them in 2023. Here's why and what to do," *Primary Care Cures*, November 11, 2022, accessed September 13, 2023, https://www. primarycarecures.com/2022/11/11/episode-184-ann-richardson-is-the-docwhisperer-she-is-letting-the-bigs-know-a-frontline-exodus-is-hitting-them-in-2023-heres-why-and-what-to-do/.

She points out that there's a "code of silence that goes on in medicine, which is dangerous medicine. Because if patients don't have a voice, and if they were to know the doctors and nurses didn't have a voice, that's as dangerous as it gets for the sick."

These egregious circumstances are eliminated when a doctor extricates themselves from the mainstream system. Doctors working via direct-pay or subscription-pay have the freedom to truly impact their patients' lives for the better—which is likely the motivation that led them to become doctors in the first place.

In a future where direct-pay services are standard, doctors have a robust roster of patients. They see roughly 1 percent of those patients per day, and they are able to take time with them. Sufficient income is arriving regularly. They are able to pay their office costs, necessary maintenance and insurance fees, and medical school loans and still maintain a good living.

DPC SPECIALIZATION

Future development in the direct-pay community would include DPC doctor specialization. Currently, most DPC physicians do not specialize in geriatrics, and they shy away from high-risk age groups. However, as we discussed, this type of care is ideal for the geriatric patient. This DPC Sherpa would be familiar with Medicare and how to help their patients take the best advantage of the resources they offer. The need for qualified, compassionate physicians to take time with these patients is present and ever-growing.

Along a similar line, DPC doctors with staff who can help our veterans navigate the Veterans Affairs are in great demand. Again, the time and attention DPC doctors provide their patients would cause this group to thrive. In the future, I hope that this model becomes the norm for our elderly and veterans.

RADIOLOGY

The high prices of x-rays and ultrasounds can be drastically cut in the future by using the medical training facilities at community colleges all over the nation. Qualified radiology technician instructors ensure the quality of the imaging, the next generation of radiology technicians are learning necessary processes, and full studies can result at a fraction of the cost of traditional imaging centers.

I am exploring how to create community imaging centers in hospital-dominated cites where the hospitals will not collaborate with us to hold down costs. What could be done with the unused time in a state-of-the-art community college training facility? Many federally qualified health centers and not-for-profit clinics offer imaging, and these resources can be tapped as well. In fact, a clinic that I staff in Houston offers automated breast ultrasound, something not even offered at many hospitals. My vision is to pull together the stakeholders in the community and add additional modalities needed. Scores of patients who otherwise couldn't afford the studies they need, as well as employers struggling under the weight of egregious healthcare costs, would have access to affordable, state-of-the-art care.

Employers

The future that is possible for employers is, perhaps, the most dramatic. Employers are drowning in mainstream insurance demands that grow worse with each passing year. A future where these demands are brought under control is possible.

In this setting, employers are doing their fiduciary duty and providing outstanding healthcare that is far less expensive than that of the traditional, mainstream system. They have direct-pay or subscription-pay contracts with DPC doctors, specialists, radiologists, and hospitals to get their employees the care they need. Outstanding catastrophic coverage is set and ready for emergencies, and anything else is billed and paid for on a monthly basis—at drastically reduced, contracted rates, of course. The stress and uncertainty of providing healthcare have been eliminated. Costs are manageable, and the finance department can more accurately foresee their next years' profits. They will pass these profits on to employees via wage increases. Workers, in return, are satisfied employees who enjoy improved health and positivity regarding coming to work each day.

We are currently experiencing an unprecedented crisis in the US workforce.

Employers, in some cases, are desperate to find and retain qualified talent, just as they were in the days of the Civil War. A September 2023 article from the US Chamber of Commerce, "Understanding America's Labor Shortage," says this:

> We hear every day from our member companies—of every size and industry, across nearly every state—they're facing unprecedented challenges trying to find enough workers to fill open jobs. Right now, the latest data shows that we have 9.8 million job openings in the United States, but only 5.9 million unemployed workers.

> The US Chamber surveyed unemployed workers who lost their jobs during the pandemic on what is keeping them from returning to work. Twenty-seven percent indicated that the need to be home and care for children or other family members has made the return to work difficult or impossible. More than a quarter (28%) indicated that they have

been ill and their health has taken priority over looking for work.[65]

With these types of unique challenges, employers must be more strategic than ever in their attempts to find talent and keep employees over the long term. Let's face it; most people work for two reasons alone: money and benefits—period. Offering comprehensive healthcare and steady wage increases is the way to keep employees and ensure their satisfaction with their employment. When employees are happy at their job, they want to be there, obviously resulting in less absenteeism. Employees who feel cared for by their employer show more engaged participation, and they are generally satisfied employees.

Like Harris Rosen did in the past, employers in this future create work environments that are safe, healthy, and promote camaraderie and a sense of belonging. Their employees are happy, in good health, and in good spirits, and they're dedicated, productive team members.

The Patient

Of course, the patient is of most importance in the direct-pay model. In the future I envision, no one is denied healthcare. It's affordable, patients are getting outstanding support from their DPC doctors, and health insurance limitations are a thing of the past.

People are taking their health seriously; they are eating strategically for optimum health, and exercise is encouraged as *necessary care*. Prescriptions aren't needed nearly as much, but when they are, they're

---

65 Stephanie Ferguson, "Understanding America's labor shortage," U.S. Chamber of Commerce, September 11, 2023, accessed September 17, 2023, https://www. uschamber.com/workforce/understanding-americas-labor-shortage.

affordable, if not completely free, through their employer and/or DPC doctor's Sherpa-style guidance. In the event of an emergency care need, patients are not thrown into panic because of looming debt. They have a secure catastrophic policy to depend on.

The elderly, veterans, and Medicare populations would be cared for with outstanding DPC services. In fact, they would thrive because their DPC physician pays attention to their needs, and importantly, these groups receive assistance with the resources that are available to them. In this future, healthcare encourages "caring for the patient's health."

This isn't just a dream; this vision is already a reality for some. In Houston, we're blessed to have Next Level Urgent Care, Green Imaging, and Texas Medical Management, which is a bundled surgery program, all working together. A huge percentage of patient care, and an equally huge percentage of patient cost, is slashed when combining these three resources. The facilities and staff have established workflows, they know how to work together efficiently, and each has a mutual interest in the patient's well-being. This gives patients in Houston a seamless path to direct-pay care.

In both the Houston and the Katy, Texas, areas, there is another reality of outstanding care for patients' health at costs people of all socioeconomic circumstances can afford: Christ Clinic. With Executive Director Lara Mautz, RN, at the helm, Christ Clinic sees fifteen thousand appointments a year; everything is $0 out-of-pocket for those patients falling below 200 percent of the poverty line; they have specialists of all kinds that come in to see patients in the clinic; and pharmaceuticals are offered at free or greatly reduced prices, as the clinic participates in a low-cost program that provides generic equivalents of most medications for pennies on the dollar. Christ Clinic also offers its services as DPC to employers in the area.

We're proving in the private sector that direct-pay healthcare, including a subscription-based DPC doctor, provides the patient with superior results. The needs of each primary group affected by healthcare are met—doctors, employers, and patients—when utilizing the direct-pay model. It's an outstanding way to practice medicine, and in the future, I see this seamless, low-cost medical care as the norm rather than the exception.

Contact Me

Feel free to follow me on LinkedIn at https://www.linkedin.com/in/cristin-dickerson-md-a1a1b013/ or email me at drdickerson@green-imaging.net.

I speak nationally on the pursuit of healthcare value. As a Health Rosetta advisor, I can serve as chief medical officer and/or advise on employer-funded health plans. I also am happy to find imaging options for not-for-profit clinics and community health plans. I look forward to a day when this book becomes obsolete, and the ecosystem I have watched grow over the last decade is the mainstream system!

BONUS CONSOLIDATED RESOURCES

ORGANIZATIONS PROMOTING AFFORDABLE EMPLOYER-FUNDED HEALTH PLANS	
Aspirational Healthcare	aspirationalhealthcare.com
Health Benefits Nation by Validation Inst.	healthbenefitsnation.com
Health Rosetta	healthrosetta.org
Mitigate Partners	mitigatepartners.com
NextGen Benefits	nextgenbenefits.com
E-powered Benefits & YOU Powered Symposium	epoweredbenefits.com
Free Market Medical Association	fmma.org
ATTORNEYS FAMILIAR WITH DPC LEGALITIES	
DPC Frontier	dpcfrontier.com
Chris Deacon	https://www.linkedin.com/in/chrisdeaconesq/

BENEFITS ADVISORS	
Health Rosetta	healthrosetta.org
NextGen Benefits	nextgenbenefits.com
E-powered Benefits & YOU Powered Symposium	epoweredbenefits.com
Mitigate Partners	mitigatepartners.com
Validation Institute Certified	validationinstitute.com

BOOKS	
Marshall Allen	*Never Pay the First Bill and Other Ways to Fight the Healthcare System and Win*
Dave Chase	*The COVID-19 Wake-Up Call, Relocalizing Health: The Future of Healthcare Is Local, Open, and Independent*
Tony Dale	*The Cure For Healthcare: An Old-World Doctor's Prescription for the New World Health System*
Nelson L. Griswold	*Breaking through the Status Quo: How Innovative Companies Are Changing the Benefits Game to Help Their Employees and Boost Their Bottom Line*

DPC CONFERENCES	
AAFP DPC Summit	dpcsummit.org
Docs 4 Patient Care Foundation DPC Nuts & Bolts Conference	d4pcfoundation.com
The Hint Summit	summit.hint.com
E-powered Benefits & YOU Powered Symposium	epoweredbenefits.com

PATIENT ADVOCACY	
Graith Care	graithcare.com
Cynthia Fisher, Patient Rights Advocate	patientrightsadvocate.org

PHYSICIAN-FOUNDED RETAIL HEALTHCARE PURCHASING OPTIONS	
Green Imaging	greenimaging.net
Surgery Center of Oklahoma	surgerycenterok.com
Texas Medical Management	texasmedicalmanagement.com
UberDoc	uber-docs.co

SECULAR HEALTH-SHARING OPTIONS	
Sedera	sedera.com
Zion HealthShare	zionhealth.org

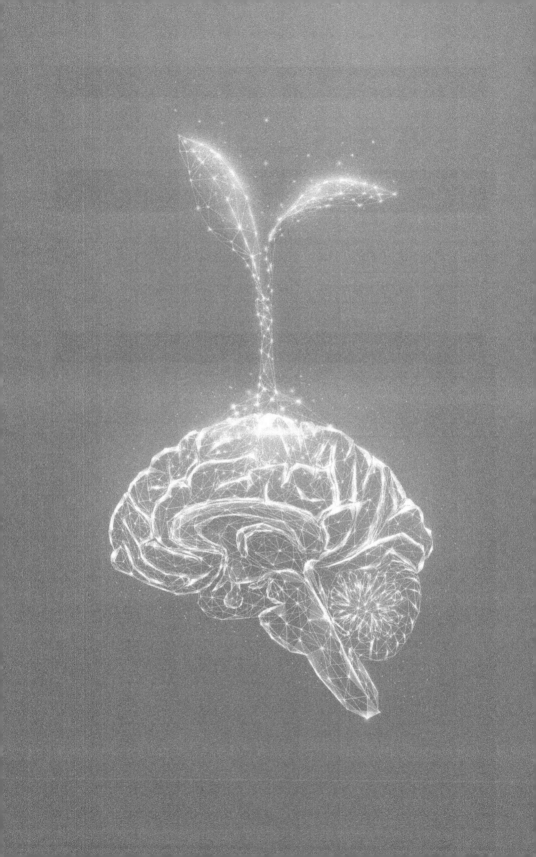

ABOUT THE AUTHOR

Cristin Dickerson, MD, is a practicing radiologist and a lifetime Texan. She trained at UT Medical School at Houston, now McGovern Medical School at UT Health, where she was a chief resident and graduated with honors. She was a two-term managing partner of a Texas Medical Center multispecialty group and oversaw a self-funded health plan for over three hundred employees. Her older son is a healthcare analyst in Austin, and her younger son, who has Angelman syndrome, lives at home with his parents. She is an avid tennis player and enjoys weekend hikes in the Texas Hill Country. She and her husband founded Green Imaging in 2011 as a family business to solve a community problem, and they've turned it into a national solution for employer health plans. Dr. Dickerson speaks nationally on making healthcare affordable and accessible for all Americans.

Printed in the USA
CPSIA information can be obtained
at www.ICGtesting.com
JSHW081735120224
57198JS00009B/955

9 781642 257175